AI & You

How to Think, Transform, and Thrive in an Artificial Intelligence Future

Raj Ramesh, PhD
www.topsigma.com

AI & You: How to Think, Transform, and Thrive in an Artificial Intelligence Future

www.topsigma.com

Project Managed with AuthorDock.com

ISBN: 978-1629671543
Library of Congress Control Number: 2019907901

Rev 8.11

DEDICATION

To my late father, Dr. B. Nagarajan, who inspired me to be my best, to all my teachers in life, and to my loving family

CONTENTS

INTRODUCTION
WHAT'S THIS BOOK ABOUT?

"If I were given an hour in which to do a problem upon which my life depended, I would spend 40 minutes studying it, 15 minutes reviewing it and 5 minutes solving it."

—Albert Einstein

This book is to help you adapt to the fast-changing environment around you.

Artificial intelligence (AI) is becoming pervasive. We can see and experience it when we type in a search term on Google, interact with a customer service bot at AT&T, or take a test drive in a Tesla.

We will feel the impact of AI more than the impact of the internet. This technology will be everywhere and will fundamentally change how we work and how we live.

How can you adapt to this monumental change? That is a question I will answer in this book.

In Part I, I share some ideas on the changes in technology you see around you, especially AI. These changes will drastically impact your work and personal life.

In Part II, I introduce some simple tools you could use to model the changes that are happening around you. If you model the changes, then you can understand them better.

In Part III, I show you ways to use these tools to adapt to the changes. The better you adapt to the changes, the better your future will be.

In this book, I freely borrow techniques and tools from multiple disciplines including AI, machine learning, pattern recognition, computer vision, neural networks, mathematics, statistics, data management, business strategy, engineering, computer science, software engineering, configuration modeling, business management, process optimization, system dynamics, scientific research, visual communication, and storytelling.

I hope to convince you that you have no option but to adapt to the change.

PART I: BE AWARE—HOW PERVASIVE IS AI?

1. Will You Lose Your Job?

Not too far back, a Japanese insurance company replaced thirty-four of its white-collar workers with a machine. These employees were underwriting insurance, a job that was thought to be safe from automation.

Technology is advancing fast. Think of what you do at work. Is there a chance that one day your job will be done by a machine? If a machine does your job, what will you be doing?

If you understand what's going on around you, then you can take action and be in a better position when, not if, the day comes that you are replaced.

For this reason, it's imperative that you figure it out, and figure it out quickly.

Since every job is different, I cannot offer you guidance on your particular occupation. However, I can offer you a framework and the tools to evaluate your specific situation and take steps.

Technology can drive change, but improved technology alone is not enough to bring about change. Many other factors, such as an accepting business environment, the mindsets of the people in your workplace, and financial incentives, contribute to the success of change. Take the example of the simple computer keyboard layout.

We should have adapted to the DVORAK keyboard from the QWERTY keyboard. The latter was created at a time when typewriters were mechanical devices, and the placement of keys was intentionally designed so that the type heads wouldn't hit each other. However, since the time when this constraint was removed with the advent of digital keyboards, we have not succeeded in switching to a system such as the DVORAK, which is designed based on the frequency of characters in common English to make typing faster.

More Machines and Fewer People

On September 19, 1977, a day now called Black Monday, the Campbell Works of Youngstown Sheet and Tube shut its doors, leaving about 5,000 people out of a job. This was just the beginning, as other steel mills started to shut down. The mills had failed to modernize, and the technological revolution essentially pulverized jobs in its path as it swept through Youngstown.[1] Following the crisis, in 1981 U.S. Steel offered $6.3 billion for the Marathon Oil Company. That sum would have built a new steel mill or paid for the modernization of U.S. Steel's existing facilities. Why did a leading firm of an industry desperately needing modernization decide to buy an oil company instead? Because change is difficult; it's much easier to pursue an alternate path, such as buying a company in the hopes of reinventing yourself, than to change yourself.

Here's a back-of-the-napkin comparison with U.S. steel showing that technology increases productivity and therefore affects employment. As of 2019, the largest company in the U.S., Apple, is worth $1 trillion and employs about 132,000 people. This means that Apple is worth twenty times what U.S. Steel is worth, yet with a third as many employees[2]—a factor of sixty in productivity!

In the modern era, Microsoft is working on an AI algorithm that can

---

[1] Staughton Lynd, "Big Steel's Irony; Youngstown," *The New York Times*, December 1, 1981, Opinion, http://www.nytimes.com/1981/12/01/opinion/big-steel-s-irony-youngstown-ohio-us-steel-has-offered-6.3-billion-for-marathon.html.
[2] Len Bolsevic, "Steel Standing: U.S. Steel celebrates 100 years," *Post Gazette,* February 25, 2001, http://old.post-gazette.com/businessnews/20010225ussteel2.asp.

write code.[3] Even now, many parts of a computer program can be generated automatically with a few high-level instructions. Because of changing technologies like this one, white-collar jobs in software development, accounting, legal, hospitality, finance, and many more industries will be augmented by or in some cases replaced by machines. The utopian view is that man and machine will work together to substantially increase productivity, but the reality is that many skills will eventually be outdated. Just like industrial automation made some skills obsolete, the age of cognition, when machines can function autonomously, will make many skills obsolete. Now is the time to prepare for this change.

It is not all doom and gloom, though. Yes, some jobs will be lost, but perhaps many more will be created, as history has shown repeatedly. The key is to skill or reskill yourself to be in a better position. To do that, first you have to understand what is happening around you, then build a mindset to accept change, and then actually change.

Any sufficiently advanced technology is indistinguishable from magic.

—Arthur C Clarke

Like most people, you might be both excited and anxious about the future. I know I am.

I'm anxious because I don't know what the future holds. If you had told someone a hundred years ago that people would someday be able to have a face-to-face conversation via live video with others halfway across the world, few would have believed or even understood you. Likewise, few can envision—and no one can predict—what the world will be like a hundred years from now. Given that the current pace of technology is accelerating,[4] humanity

---

[3] Dave Gershgorn, "Microsoft's AI Is Learning to Write Code by Itself, Not Steal It," *Quartz*, accessed March 9, 2017, https://qz.com/920468/artificial-intelligence-created-by-microsoft-and-university-of-cambridge-is-learning-to-write-code-by-itself-not-steal-it/.

[4] Alison E. Berman and Jason Dorrier, "Technology Feels Like It's Accelerating—Because It Actually Is," *Singularity Hub* (blog), March 22, 2016, https://singularityhub.com/2016/03/22/technology-feels-like-its-accelerating-

will experience much more change in the next hundred years than in the previous century.

I'm excited because I know that there will be many opportunities for growth and to improve human lives. It could be the best time to live on this planet. Perhaps in the next hundred years and beyond we will be disease-free; we will live a lot longer; machines will be our friends and help us in many ways; we will know more about the edges of the universe; we will travel to distant galaxies; we will not have wars because the universe will offer its vast resources; and everything will be fantastic. It'll be Utopia!

FIGURE 1-1. Used with permission

Too Much Information

Data is growing at a tremendous pace, generated by an increasing amount of internet content, social media posts, digital photos, texting

---

because-it-actually-is/.

and other digital communication, service provider data granularity such as weather and transportation data, and the Internet of Things (IoT) devices that are attached to many appliances.

Today's business leaders are inundated with information. It's overwhelming. How do you make sense of it all? For example, if you Google the term "digital transformation," you'll get millions of results (26.5 million results, to be exact, when I checked on December 20, 2018 at 2:00 pm CST). Information is not a problem; information overload is. When so much information is thrown at us, some of us organize it better than others. Depending on how we organize it, each of us makes different decisions with the same information. How do we ensure that our decisions are the best we could be making?

FIGURE 1-2. Used with permission

The value of data is not in the volume of information, but in its essence. Machines like IBM Watson can consume large volumes of information, "reading" a million books a second.[5] But humans still need a different mechanism to consume and act on information. How can we do that?

Humans create mental models when we want to understand something. In this book, we will formalize these mental models somewhat so they are more explicit. With the help of these models, we can then organize, catalog, process, consume, and understand vast troves of information—and by doing so, we can make better decisions.

How do you create your own informal mental models? Since I believe that AI will play a strong role in tomorrow's organizations, I will use this technology to illustrate how your organization and your role in it may change in the near future. First, we have to understand how AI will be integrated into your organization and what impact it will have. Only then can we talk about the impact it will have on your role within your organization.

Neither is this a step-by-step; nor do I offer a template for you to get to the "answer." However, I will walk you through ways to build models that in turn should help you understand things around you.

You may tailor these ideas and concepts for your specific situation.

Super Convergence

Not only are current technologies advancing rapidly, but new technologies are also being developed every day. These technologies interact with one another, and you can't really consider any of them in isolation.

I present a concept called *super convergence* in a five-minute video. If you are reading this book in electronic form, you can click or tap on the image to get to the video. If you are reading this book in paper form, you can scan the QR code below with your mobile device. There are several videos throughout the book presented in the same

---

[5] "Artificial Intelligence Positioned to Be a Game-Changer," *CBS News*, October 9, 2016, http://www.cbsnews.com/news/60-minutes-artificial-intelligence-charlie-rose-robot-sophia/.

way.

The idea is that when a business tries to incorporate a new technology into its operations—for the purposes of improving customer experiences, improving operational effectiveness, or developing the right products—it has to consider multiple technologies simultaneously to identify which fit what situation, and how they can be integrated to work well with one another.

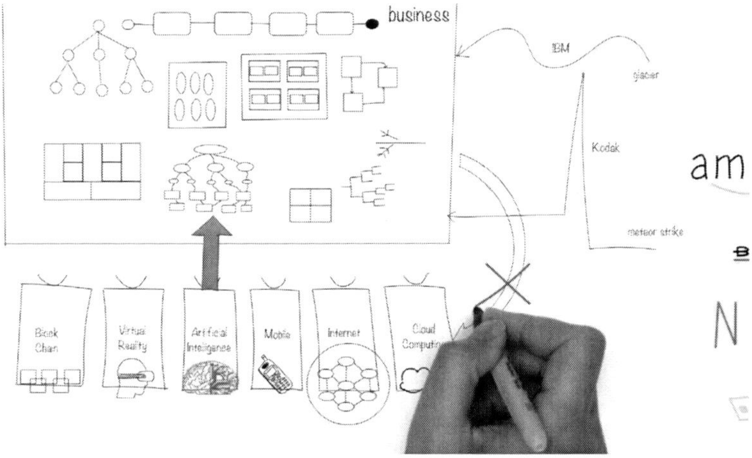

Video: super convergence of technologies

As the video illustrates, an organization is a complex entity, and your role in that organization requires interaction with this complexity. It is crucial for you to understand your environment before you respond to your organization's internal and external changes. To answer the original question we posed, "Will you lose your job?" the answer is, "Not if you recognize the changes happening around you and adapt to those changes effectively."

2. How Technology Is Changing Business and Why to Care

Two engineering students founded the company Research in Motion in 1985. This company developed the famous BlackBerry device, which was the precursor of the smartphone. In the late 90s and early 2000s, Research in Motion was one of the most valuable technology companies in the world. Now, it's well past its heyday.[6]

Change is not a question of if, but when. Even the largest companies can change or disappear. So can whole civilizations and superpowers. You too should expect change. Change in the business world can be driven by shifts in customer expectations, the invention of new and disruptive technologies, new competitors, and more. As you think about your own work ecosystem, it is important to understand what changes are happening.

Given the breadth of possibilities, in this book we are going to only discuss the changes driven by disruptive technologies. Again, technology is just one factor that you can model in order to better understand change. You could extend the modeling to include other drivers of change as well, and that should become clear by the time you finish the book.

Technology Driving Change

Technology is evolving at a fast pace. You may remember the rise and fall of Pokémon Go in 2016, which was but a blip on the timescale. Few are talking about it now, but for several months the game was disrupting normal life.

A few decades ago, no one could have anticipated some of the business models of today. Uber threatens to overshadow the rest of

---

[6] Rod McQueen, *BlackBerry: The Inside Story of Research in Motion* (Key Porter Books, 2010).

the taxi market[7] and yet it owns very few cars. Airbnb has more room listings than the largest hotel chains and yet it owns very few properties.[8] Netflix is the largest TV streaming service and yet it owns no theaters. Facebook is the largest content sharing company and yet it produces little original content.

Applications like Spotify and products like Roomba are using technology to establish new business models. Pokémon Go did too, but quickly disappeared. The old notion of "first define the business, then figure out the technologies to enable that business" is not applicable anymore. Tomorrow's business models will be created based on the technology that is available then.

Now when a new technology emerges people figure out how to implement it in new business models. We have seen this time and time again. Without the internet, Amazon would not have been conceived of, much less thrived. Without the smartphone, Uber would not have been possible.

---

[7] Henry Blodget, "Uber CEO Reveals Mind-Boggling New Statistic That Skeptics Will Hate," *Business Insider*, accessed April 24, 2017, http://www.businessinsider.com/uber-revenue-san-francisco-2015-1.

[8] Rolfe Winkler and Douglas MacMillan, "The Secret Math of Airbnb's $24 Billion Valuation," *Wall Street Journal*, June 17, 2015, Tech, https://www.wsj.com/articles/the-secret-math-of-airbnbs-24-billion-valuation-1434568517.

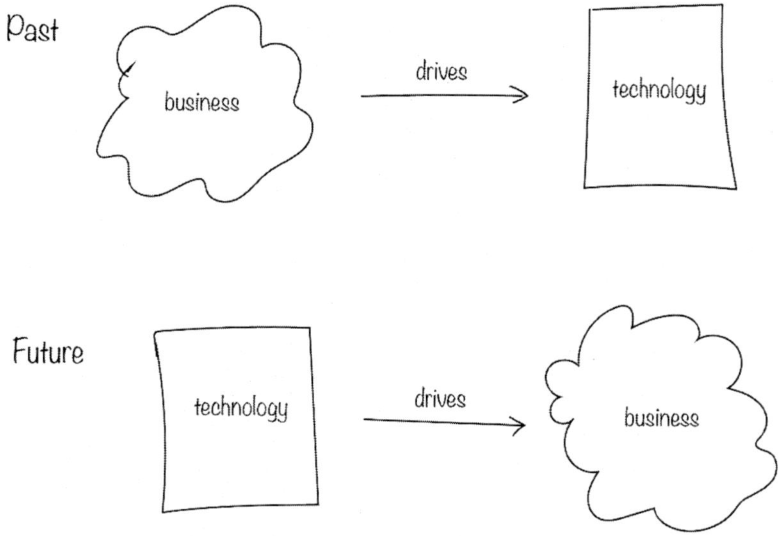

FIGURE 2-1: Technology drives business models

New business models have been born, not of a single technology but of an intelligent interweaving of multiple technologies. These technologies include cloud computing, social networks, IoT, mobile devices, AI, blockchain, and virtual reality (VR), among others. Using innovative business models, new entrants to the market are posing a severe threat to incumbents, many of which have been too slow to adjust. These newer companies are doing the equivalent of *unbundling* the monolithic companies—in other words, breaking up the functions of the larger companies into smaller units that can be rearranged in innovative ways. Likewise, many new and disruptive technologies will be integrated into new companies and coexist with old and yet-to-be-invented technologies. This is another example of super convergence.

Technology permeates business today; the two are tightly integrated. In fact, the lines between business and technology are becoming blurry. Because technology is so integral to business, leaders must know how to leverage it in their organizations. They need to understand what any given technology can or cannot do; how it works; how it can be combined with other technologies; what its impact is on the other elements of the organization such as processes, people, and data; how competitors may leverage it to their advantage; and how to integrate it into the organization.

Some business models such as those of Amazon and Google are entirely based on technology—if you took away the technology, there would be no business. Companies such as Airbnb and Uber would not exist if the technology to facilitate their transactions were not available. Some companies like Southwest Airlines, on the other hand, use technology—particularly the internet—to enhance their existing business models and adapt along the way. Southwest Airlines started with the only relevant technology available at the time: the telephone. Then it adapted to the internet and mobile devices.

Tesla is able to offer cars directly to its customers by leveraging the internet, whereas legacy auto companies such as GM and Ford are forced to sell their cars through dealers. As you can imagine, it is difficult to change that business model by taking dealers out of the equation. Because Tesla has a direct relationship with its customers with no go-betweens, it can understand their behaviors and expectations faster and adapt quickly, while saving the cost of the intermediaries. In fact, it is able to send direct software updates to its cars wirelessly to identify and fix problems. Tesla has gathered over 1.2 million miles of autopilot data, which if harnessed correctly can offer a huge competitive advantage.[9]

For yet another example, consider insurance. Traditional insurance providers sell through their agents, but newer business models like Lemonade sell directly to the customer. You might think that insurance is a complicated product, but with technologies like AI, machines may eventually be able to do most of the work. Then what happens?

As more technology becomes available, more business models are possible. In the future, even more advanced technologies may supersede the current business models of Amazon and Facebook.

---

[9] Fred Lambert, "Tesla's fleet has accumulated over 1.2 billion miles on Autopilot and even more in 'shadow mode', report says," *Elektrek,* July 17th, 2018, https://electrek.co/2018/07/17/tesla-autopilot-miles-shadow-mode-report/.

Having given some examples of how technology drives change, I'd like to emphasize that technology by itself is not the only factor. Technology exists within the context of a whole system, and some parts of the system may have to change to accommodate the technology. In this battle, sometimes technology loses, or at least its adoption is postponed.

Other factors in the system may deter change, and the best technology does not always win. This is due to the strength of the underlying system and the network that a company could be a part of. In the case of GM, its distributers are going to fight tooth and nail to keep their business models. Social and political battles will have to be fought and won before direct relationships with customers will become more common for traditional automobile companies.

As another example, consider the U.S. tax system. Transitioning to a flat tax system would be extremely difficult, because there are so many parties that form an integral part of the current system and have a strong vested interest in it. These parties include accountants, tax consultants, tax software creators, and even the IRS. A lot of people could potentially lose their jobs if the U.S. transitions to a flat tax system. In this hypothetical example, even though we have the technology to change, the overall system may resist.

Challenges to Integrating Technology into Business

Years before the smartphone, Apple came up with the Newton, which was a handheld device intended to track your calendar, appointments, and notes. By today's standards it was rudimentary, but at the time, the technology was at the cutting edge.[10] The technology itself might have been accepted, but after a well-known cartoonist derided it for being an overpriced paper notebook and Steve Jobs made his distaste of it known, the project was terminated.

---

[10] "Remembering the Apple Newton's Prophetic Failure and Lasting Impact," Mat Honan, *Wired Magazine,* August 05, 2013, https://www.wired.com/2013/08/remembering-the-apple-newtons-prophetic-failure-and-lasting-ideals/.

Factors other than technology caused its rejection in the marketplace. This again shows that the integration of technology into an organization is not only a technological issue. Rather, it requires changes along multiple dimensions such as social acceptance, organizational structure, business processes, vendor relationships, and employee functions.

When the iPhone was released years later, it gained wide acceptance quickly, primarily due to two reasons: (1) people had been exposed to new forms of digital technology by that time and were ready and (2) the technology had improved so much that there was less friction and more ease of use. Making the best use of this acceptance by users, Apple was able to build a full ecosystem of connections among its devices and applications—like the iMac, Apple Watch, iTunes, etc.

Many new and disruptive technologies are continuing to emerge. These or combinations of these will be harnessed in new business models. Let's look at some of the potential challenges.

The following picture shows some of the technologies that may impact your company and your life:

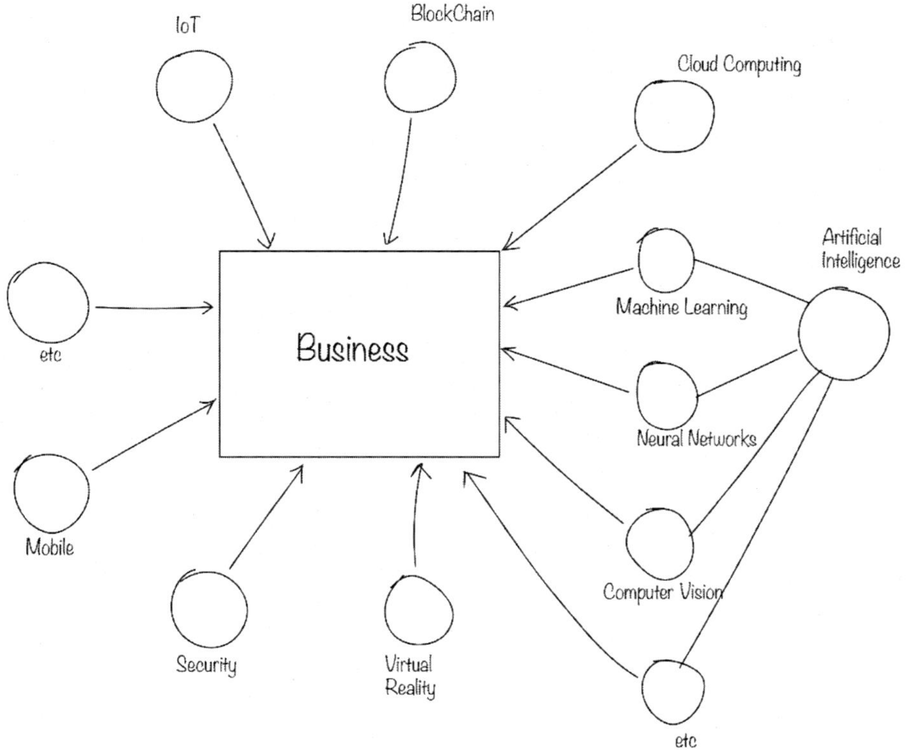

FIGURE 2-2: Technologies that drive business changes

Integrating these technologies into an existing business model is a herculean task. When integrating technologies, it's necessary to think about the future: what is going to happen ten or twenty years from now. One of the best approaches is to start from scratch, but most companies do not have that option or flexibility. Only a few companies, such as Google, are able to pull it off. The existing context and ecosystem have to be considered, and we have to work within those constraints.

The viable alternative is to understand your existing industry to the extent that you can figure out how to effectively adjust to super convergence of the technology and transformation of your business. This requires an engineering approach to designing your own future. The principles of such an engineering approach are what I will discuss in the later chapters, with a specific focus on the integration of AI.

Adjusting to AI

Many of the ways businesses operate will change in the next five years, and we have to adapt now.

As I mentioned earlier, we will be inundated by data as the volume of information continues to grow quickly. AI will be the ideal technology to consume this data and "learn" from it. For this reason, it will become an integral part of most organizations. As most businesses' processes are infused with some form of AI, they will undergo massive disruption. But, just like we have gotten used to technologies such as computers and the internet, we will get used to AI.

Many business processes will have intelligence built into them so as to react to a dynamic ecosystem and varying customer needs. Traditionally, categories of customers were segmented into large groups. Now, with the power of data and intelligence, customers are increasingly being treated and catered to as individuals. Organizations and their processes are being driven to be nimble and adapt to each customer's unique needs.

Humans and machines will be collaborating at new levels, complementing their respective strengths to solve big problems. Businesses will need to construct the ecosystem that makes this collaboration possible. To construct such an ecosystem, they must first understand everything that needs to be in it.

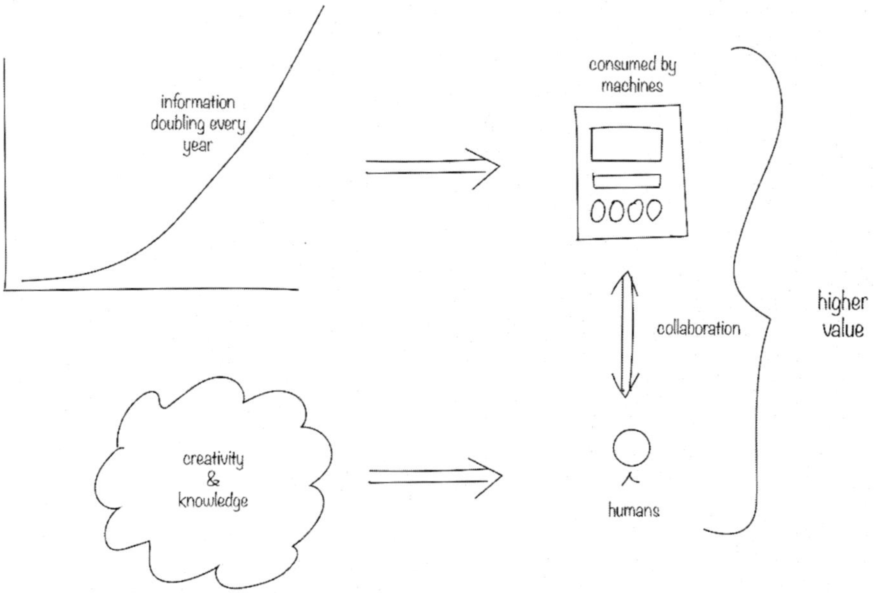

Figure 2-3: Human-machine collaboration

If you were planning a camping trip, you'd list the things that you would have to pack—tent, sleeping bags, stove, etc.—depending on a number of internal and external factors, such as how far the camping site was from a grocery store, what the weather was going to be like, how much water you would need to store, whether you would have to worry about wild animals, and so on.

This is essentially similar to planning for the business ecosystem, but there are a few differences. One is scale. A business is much larger than a campsite. Another is coordinating decision-making responsibilities among multiple people. If one person or group of people were responsible for providing the "tent" and another the "pegs," you would want to make sure that the pegs were suitable for the type of tent procured. In the real world, this is a bigger challenge than you'd think. There is no "enterprise checklist" that's comparable to a camping list. As you can see, the more "stuff" and constraints you add, the bigger the challenge—but it can be done.

To summarize, technology is driving fundamental changes in business. In fact, it is difficult to find a business today that in some way is not driven by technology. Businesses will continue to leverage technology for their operations and competitive advantage. If you want to adapt to and thrive in the business environment of the future, you need to understand how technology, and especially AI, can impact your life.

3. How Will Your Role Change?

Your life today is probably a lot different from what it was like a couple of decades ago. Today, you can videoconference with your parents in France from the Grand Canyon using a small device. This device also acts as a personal assistant, phone, shopping list, and idea notebook, and it allows you to connect to work, to name a few capabilities. The things that you interact with today are much different from the things that your great-grandmother interacted with. Basically, the world around you is constantly changing and will continue to change. Your world is the "stuff" that surrounds you and impacts your life. We will call this stuff *elements*.

Let's make this more concrete with the camping example I shared in the last chapter. When you are camping, the elements that you interact with include the campsite, the facilities, the neighboring town, your campground neighbors, the tools you have, your food, etc. It might also include the organization that manages the campground; the governing bodies that establish rules at the local, state, and federal levels; vendors, etc. Essentially all these elements make the campground and camping feasible. The better you understand these elements and how to interact with them, the better your camping experience will be. For example, you might have to make a reservation for the campsite with the Parks and Recreation Department before you can camp. When you plan for and go camping, you are operating within a system, which we shall call the *camping ecosystem*.

Now let's look at another ecosystem—your *work ecosystem*. An ecosystem is a virtual grouping of all the elements that are included in a specific context. If you work in an office as an employee at a company, the elements that you interact with may include things like your coworkers, the tools you use, your desk, your computer, other machines, customers, their expectations, competitors, the company culture, management, business processes that you interact with, and so on. In other words, you are operating within a complex system, interacting with various elements. Just like your camping experience will be better if you understand how to interact with the elements in your camping ecosystem, your job and your future will be better if you have a good understanding of how to interact with the elements in your business. If you can anticipate the changes to that ecosystem, then you will be prepared for the changes to your own work that come with them.

Driven by changes, your role within your organization and your organization's role within the world will continue to evolve. Some of the questions we'll try to answer are: Will your organization be able to adapt to the new changes? If it can adapt, what will your role be in the transformed organization? How will the organization itself flourish in the new ecosystem? If it cannot adapt, how will you position yourself then? What are the changes you need to make on a personal level, independent of the organizational direction?

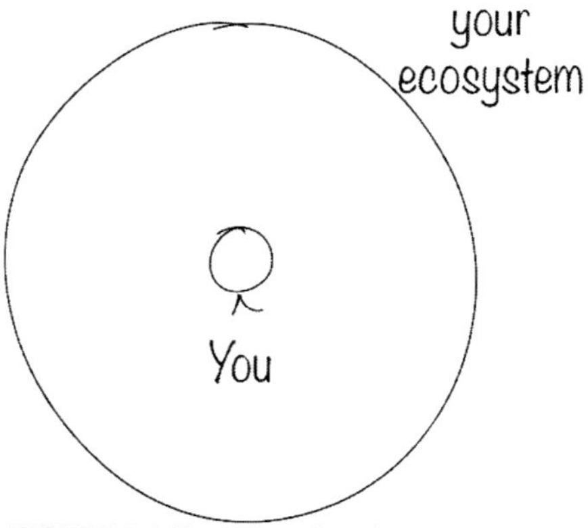

FIGURE 3-1: Depiction of you in your ecosystem

These are two things to consider: (1) your organization's future and (2) your future.

You will likely have a different ecosystem than a colleague, even though you both work in the same department in the same company. That's because you may never have to interact with a system that they are interacting with or may never interact with a manager that they have to interact with. Incidentally, you don't have to identify all the elements in your ecosystem to be able to understand it.

Charging into the future will be a transformational journey, both for yourself as an individual and for your organization. The only difference is the scale of the transformation. For you to change personally, you have to convince yourself and drive change within your ecosystem. For your organization to change, it has to convince most of its employees and drive the same change within a larger ecosystem. Since there are a lot more elements and connections among those elements in an organization, the change itself will be more complex, but the fundamental concepts are the same.

Consider the organization you work for. It may have physical locations or be virtual. It has many elements that interact with one another to produce value for its clients, including processes, people, technology, and resources. Your organization is also affected by many elements outside itself, including vendors, competitors, laws, and customers.

This picture reflects your organizational ecosystem and the elements in it. You have a place in this ecosystem, and if you understand that place, you can adapt and thrive. You can even go further and drive change in that ecosystem: change that you want to see. This is one way to make a difference!

How Will Change Impact You?

FIGURE 3-2: How will change impact you?

What do you think will change in your ecosystem? Here are some possibilities that are by no means exhaustive. If you can understand and model a few of these, then you will be able to think through, model, and understand new situations:

- An executive wants to explore a new technology to see how it can be leveraged.
- A competitor with a new business model seems to be grabbing market share away from your company.
- Your friends who work at other companies are talking about a new concept they are working on. You want to persuade the leadership at your company to explore this concept as well.
- Your former colleagues have started a new company. They want you to join them. You have to weigh the mundaneness but stability of your current job with the more exciting but unstable option.
- The local taxes have suddenly increased and more people are

migrating out of the area. As a result, your company is losing its employees. What should you do?

- Most of the projects in the company are failing, and no one knows why. How do you analyze the problem?

- Different groups within your company are doing different work and nobody has any idea how they all fit together.

- Your customers are complaining, and you are losing business. How can you help to frame the problem and fix it?

- Your company's online presence is not competitive. There is no cohesive online and social media strategy. What can you do about it?

- Your company's systems run on legacy code and it's getting more and more difficult to maintain them. Code changes are difficult; hence the IT department is not able to react to business needs quickly enough. How do you ease the pain?

- New regulations have been passed and your company needs to make changes to accommodate them. How do you take a structured approach to solving this problem?

You get the picture of possibilities.

As we move on, we will focus on organizational and personal transformation. I will often use AI as the vehicle for discussion, though the concepts of understanding, modeling, and analysis are applicable in a broader domain. This is by no means a motivational self-help book, so I will not discuss what career choices are best for you. Rather, I will share some principles of modeling that you can apply to solve practical problems and analyze your ecosystem to make changes in it—incremental or drastic.

4. The Role of AI in Your Changing Ecosystem

We are at the cusp of the cognitive revolution,[11] and we need to be prepared for it.

Throughout history, technology has helped automate work. The industrial revolution automated manufacturing processes. Machines were introduced to assembly lines, enabling companies to produce more parts with better and consistent quality. Assembly line workers still worked alongside those machines in jobs that could not be automated. Throughout this revolution, many blue-collar jobs changed, and some were lost. However, many new types of jobs were created, and people upskilled to adapt.

Then came automation in the digital revolution, and computers automated many tasks. Accountants used to spend most of their time doing calculations, but now calculators and spreadsheets automate those tasks. Modern accountants are able to spend more time analyzing results instead of computing. Many white-collar jobs changed during the digital revolution, and some were lost. However, once again, many new types of jobs were created, and people upskilled to adapt.

Now we are at the beginning of a cognitive revolution, where computing machines are becoming smarter. They can learn from their environment, improve their processes, and make decisions, at least within narrow domains. For example, a machine can automatically decide when to buy or sell a stock and can get better at it over time. In this revolution, many white-collar jobs will change, and some will be lost. However, as in the past, many new types of jobs will be created, and people will have to upskill to adapt.

---

[11] Doug Nelson, "The cognitive revolution is here, so get out of the Stone Age," *IBM,* June 23, 2017, https://www.ibm.com/information-technology/cognitive-revolution-here-so-get-out-stone-age.

The Subdisciplines of AI

AI is an umbrella term for cognitive technologies that mimic the intelligent behavior of humans, in some cases exceeding human limits.[12] These technologies will become more pervasive in organizations, while humans work alongside them.

The following video explains many of the subdisciplines that make up AI.

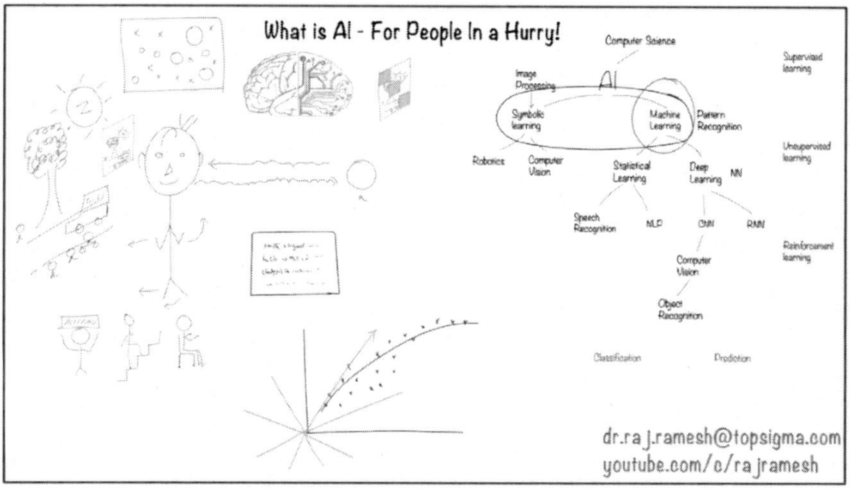

FIGURE 4-1: What is AI?

Fundamentally, think of everything that the human brain can do: its ability to recognize objects and faces, understand language, solve

---

[12] Jessica Thompson, "Artificial Intelligence: It's Not Man vs. Machine. It's Man And Machine," *Gigaom,* October 5, 2016, https://gigaom.com/2016/10/05/artificial-intelligence-its-not-man-vs-machine-its-man-and-machine/.

problems, control movement, experience emotions, etc. When AI researchers and technologists started to explore how the human brain works with the intent of creating a single system that functions like the brain, they soon realized the difficulty of such an exercise. No single system or set of algorithms was able to replicate the general functionality of the human brain.

Instead, researchers started looking at different subdisciplines to solve different problems. For example, humans can see with their eyes and recognize objects in their environment. This gave rise to the disciplines of image processing and computer vision. The goal of these disciplines was to build systems and software that could see as well as or better than humans can and could recognize objects in the scene by type.

In other words, researchers took the challenge of replicating the functions of the human brain and broke it down into narrowly focused disciplines to solve narrow problems. The ultimate idea was that once we developed and built all these individual systems, they could somehow be put together to achieve the same functions a human has. That is how we ended up with the many subdisciplines that come under the umbrella of AI.

The following is a list and brief explanation of some of these subdisciplines of AI:

- *Pattern recognition* is the science of being able to recognize patterns in data. This includes object recognition, pattern analysis in data, and handwritten character recognition.

- *Machine learning* is the science of being able to teach a computer to learn things so that it can respond to similar or new situations. This is unlike the programming paradigm where the programmer has to code all possible combinations of responses programmatically. Machine learning includes face recognition, playing games such as chess, and predicting the weather. Machine learning and pattern recognition share many algorithms.

- *Cognitive computing* is the science of problem solving, which considers many facts to come to conclusions. Cognitive computing includes logical derivations and processing lots of information to arrive at new conclusions, among other functions.

- *Robotics* is the science controlling mechanical objects in a nondeterministic environment through software. Robotics uses algorithms from other subdisciplines to react to the environment.

- *Neural networks/deep learning* is the science of replicating the neural structure of the human brain to achieve a wide range of abilities that humans are able to do. Recently this subdiscipline has been widely successful in replicating many functions of the human brain, such as being able to recognize objects and faces, learn new concepts, and even help make decisions.

- *Natural language processing* is the science of understanding and responding to human language. Applications include automated phone responses and voice-driven commands.

- *Computer vision* is the science of replicating human vision to recognize objects, see color, and identify visual patterns.

- *Image processing* is the science of processing digital images. This is often used as the first step in computer vision to process the individual pixels that make up an image. For example, to recognize an object, its outline has to first be figured out. After that, computer vision algorithms can try to decode what the outline represents. Image processing algorithms also play a major role in face recognition.

- *Associative memory* is the science of replicating the human memory on one particular aspect of recall through association. This is useful for instantaneous recall when, say, we are picking out a known face from a crowd. Traditional computer memory uses sequential scans and address references.

- *Genetic/evolutionary programming* is the science of replicating human evolution on a fast timescale so that we can hope to get improvements over much iteration.

These subdisciplines make up the overarching discipline of AI. However, these are not siloed disciplines, as they borrow techniques and algorithms from one another to achieve different objectives. For example, to train a machine to recognize a known object such as an aircraft, we would likely use algorithms and techniques from image processing, computer vision, pattern recognition, and neural networks.

Recently, neural networks and a special adaptation of it called deep learning have gained much traction because of a push from companies like Google and Facebook. Successes in this subdiscipline have also encouraged more exploration.

In essence, AI is an umbrella of many disciplines and techniques that help to not only automate, but also provide predictive and cognitive abilities. With this technology, every aspect of business and every business will be impacted.

Shifting Paradigms

Public interest in AI has been reignited after the "long winter of AI" of the 70s, 80s, and 90s.[13] Large data sets are now available for training AI systems, and computing power has increased following Moore's Law of doubling every eighteen months. With these advances, system design is changing from a programmatic paradigm to a learning paradigm. The basic paradigm shift is from writing code and business rules that control the logic flow, to one where the underlying pattern is inferred by the machine. In this new paradigm, business processes can be more flexible and adaptable.

In a programmatic paradigm, we can write down the steps for a task and then write a computer program to perform those steps. As an example, we know exactly how to balance an accounting ledger or

---

[13] The long winter of AI was triggered by the Lighthill Report, which essentially gave a negative view of AI, stating that it did not produce anything of value that it had promised. "Lighthill Report," *Wikipedia*, accessed January 30, 2016, https://en.wikipedia.org/w/index.php?title=Lighthill_report&oldid=702415961.

compute risk for issuing insurance.

In the learning paradigm, we are unable to write down a sequence of steps, and therefore cannot write a computer program to do the job. Instead, we have to find an alternate way, and that way is to use data to help the computer do the job. For example, we cannot quantify exactly how we recognize our friend's face. We just do. It's not like our brain runs through some logic to determine the distance between their eyes, the color of their eyes, their hairline, etc., to recognize them. However, if we can provide a computer many images of their face, we can eventually make the computer recognize them.

These paradigms can coexist, and businesses of the future will utilize both of them effectively. To do that, we need to understand the ecosystem of interacting systems, each of which contains one or both of the paradigms. The effective leader in the business space will be the one who leverages the right technologies in the right context.

The Impact of AI

Just as automation set the direction of business for much of the twentieth century, AI will set the direction of business for much of the twenty-first. Businesses need to know how to harness it for competitive advantage, operational efficiency, and customer intimacy.

Some fundamental business models may remain the same, but many of their components will be automated. Take call center representatives, whose responsibilities are starting to be replaced by AI technology. Machines can answer common customer questions and do so with consistency, unlike humans. This means that the call center representatives who don't lose their jobs will need to be trained to handle more complex questions and interact well with customers. Call center representatives need to understand their ecosystem to figure out what they are facing and how to adapt.

Adaptation requires us to identify the things that we humans are still better at than computers and AI.

Organizations may automate tasks well beyond answering phones. Look at other jobs in your organization that require someone to manage, process, or share data, such as the position of someone who generates data reports. This type of job can be automated. But AI systems in the organization will affect much more than these kinds of jobs; they will impact cognitive jobs as well. AI automation enables machines to do the cognitive tasks that, until now, humans have typically been better at than computers. With this shift, AI may change whole business models.

Another job currently at risk is insurance underwriting. Auto insurance underwriters, for example, consider data about the car and about the customer and consult a rating table to determine the premium they need to charge the customer. Here's a short video that demonstrates the concepts of how risk model management in insurance can be done by machines, replacing the current underwriting roles. This video also gives you a sense of how to capture and understand context—context that affects your life. I will discuss this topic in detail later.

FIGURE 4-2: Risk models using machine learning

An automated way to model risk rating will obviously displace many jobs, and the displaced people will have to be retrained. Some can be retrained and some cannot be. That's one of the implications of AI in your organization.

As you can see from the insurance underwriting example, machine learning is an AI subdiscipline of note when it comes to its impact. Machine learning replicates the cognitive abilities of humans by identifying underlying patterns and structure in data. If machines can see and recognize things in their environment, they can robotically interact with that environment. If machines can comb through lots of unstructured data to identify anomalies or patterns, they can help humans make decisions. If machines can learn new behaviors, they can adapt. Many of these possibilities exist now, and many are on the horizon. Enabling self-driving cars, automatically identifying tumors in radiology images, identifying defective parts in an assembly line, and interactive gaming are but a few of the applications of AI. Each industry can benefit from a plethora of specific AI techniques (often called narrow AI) to make business more effective.

However, AI also has to integrate with the ecosystems of humans and other technologies. Imagine an AI machine reading data from the cloud to build internal models, and then performing robotic surgery or using that information to train a surgeon with augmented reality. Different technologies would need to integrate well to provide specific, sometimes different solutions. Integration of disciplines will be critical to the business of the future. Typically, business or societal problems are not solved simply by one technology. A multidisciplinary approach is what works.

AI will alter the business landscape in complex ways in concert with other technologies like blockchain, big data, cloud computing, mobile, and VR. When an organization uses many of these technologies in aligned collaboration, the concept is called super convergence, which we explored in the first chapter.

Implications

Think about the large-scale implications. Up until now, computers could process information much faster and more consistently than humans. Now, they are beginning to think and learn like humans. While AI technologies have not yet achieved the general well-rounded knowledge and intelligence of humans, they are slowly gaining cognitive capabilities in specific narrow domains.[14]

Where does this put people like you and me? Will we reach an era of technological singularity (a hypothesis that AI will eventually surpass human intelligence and trigger runaway technological growth)?[15] It will be forty to seventy years before machines can attain many of the cognitive abilities of humans. Experts predict that

---

[14] "Zero-Shot Translation with Google's Multilingual Neural Machine Translation System," *Google Research Blog*, accessed June 20, 2017, https://research.googleblog.com/2016/11/zero-shot-translation-with-googles.html.
[15] "Technological Singularity" *Wikipedia,* accessed January 2, 2019, https://en.wikipedia.org/wiki/Technological_singularity.

the next thirty to forty years will be an era of human-machine collaboration. In this type of collaboration, humans skills will complement the capabilities of machines. Workers who will be displaced by AI need to replace their current skills with ones that will enhance this human-machine collaboration.

The continued progress in AI will complicate things, and we cannot make predictions with certainty about what skills should be learned for any specific job. Things can change in many ways. That is why my objective is to help you understand your ecosystem, so you can make those types of decisions and continue to refine and adjust your thinking as your ecosystem changes.

5. Why AI Now?

AI is ubiquitous, and in today's cultural and business climate, it is positioned for exponential growth. Netflix's movie recommendations, Amazon's product recommendations, Siri's voice recognition, Facebook's face recognition, and Google's search are all powered by AI algorithms. Many of these applications have been possible due to three main factors: (1) the availability of massive amounts of data, (2) faster computing power, and (3) the development of newer and modified algorithms.[16]

The AI discipline is in its infancy in terms of applications being developed. When software development was at this stage about thirty years ago, organizations used to develop their own custom code to automate parts of their operations. When there were enough opportunities of scale for money to be made, vendors started to develop and offer more robust products that could be purchased off the shelves or customized.

We are in a similar stage with respect to AI. Within your own industry, there may be many places where AI is applicable. Your organization will need to leverage the tools and algorithms available to start experimenting with the technology now. It cannot afford to wait for vendor-offered solutions. While some vendors will provide specific solutions for AI, you can use AI in areas of your company where vendors do not yet offer a product. When vendors do catch up, you can make the decision to either buy their solutions or use a mixed model of some vendor solutions and some in-house customization.

There is one big difference between now and thirty years ago, though. Unlike when the pace of integration of software into

---

[16] "Applications of Artificial Intelligence," *Wikipedia*, September 26, 2016, https://en.wikipedia.org/w/index.php?title=Applications_of_artificial_intelligence&oldid=741335993.

organizations was more linear, the integration of AI is expected to be exponential, which will make the pace of change much faster. This is because we have learned a lot from software implementations, and we know the benefits AI can bring. Perhaps even in the next five years, we will see big advances in AI and its integration into business.

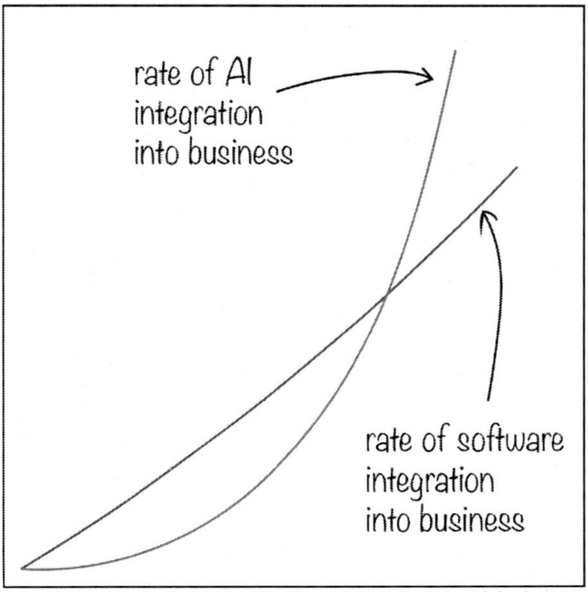

FIGURE 5-1: Rates at which software and AI are leveraged for business

The greatest shortcoming of the human race is our inability to understand the exponential function.

—Albert A. Bartlett, physicist

Further AI Implications in Business

Let's look a little deeper into the implications of AI. What happens if a new business model emerges in the same industry and space that your company operates in? This business won't have to worry about the cultural mindset or the legacy systems and processes in place. While your company may have experience and deep knowledge of the domain, the new company can make a clean start. As with anything, knowledge becomes outdated over time. To compete effectively, many elements of your company may have to be adjusted—elements like culture, systems, processes, and business models. If you can identify the elements of your business that have to be modified and develop a plan for change, you will have a fighting chance.

However, vested interests often prevent such change, even if you want it. In the last few decades we've seen what happens when new business models appear and more established businesses are unable to adjust and compete.[17]

Borders bookstore had physical locations that cost a lot of money to maintain. Expenses included rent, utilities, customer-facing employees, etc.—something Amazon did not have. Amazon, which started out as an online bookseller, displaced Borders bookstores because it used technology effectively in a new business model. Amazon could stock a much larger inventory in its warehouses since it did not have multiple retail locations. It saved on retail costs and could pass those savings on to customers. It developed an efficient distribution and shipping system. It did not have to train customer-facing employees. It tracked purchase patterns on a near-real-time basis and responded accordingly. Analytics were built into its operations from the ground up, which enabled Amazon to react quickly to changing market conditions.

Circuit City was another company that fell victim to Amazon. The money and resources invested in its physical stores was hard to recoup.

Amazon continues to disrupt not only other companies, but also itself. Many times Amazon cannibalizes its own business, such as when it allows other merchants to sell on its website (unlike its competitors like Walmart). Its website becomes a transaction medium rather than an online retail store, in which case it makes less

---

[17] Larry Downes and Paul Nunes, "Big Bang Disruption: Strategy in the Age of Devastating Innovation," *Harvard Business Review*, May 21, 2014, https://hbr.org/webinar/2014/05/big-bang-disruption-strategy-in-the-age-of-devastating-innovation.

profit per sale. Nonetheless, it seems to have successfully built a culture around the philosophy of, "If you are not moving forward, you are moving backward."

Similar to Amazon, Netflix leveraged a better business model to put Blockbuster out of business.

Uber is undoubtedly a unicorn—which happened to come up with a great business model. With this model, potentially every car becomes a cab. This completely upsets the business model of traditional cab companies. On top of this, Uber is experimenting with self-driving cars. When this becomes practically feasible in the next few years, the company can essentially be run with few people and a lot of software. While Uber is an extreme example, it is a realistic one and proves the point that tomorrow's organizations have the potential to run services primarily with machines and software instead of humans.

A few years back, travel agents used to help coordinate travel plans for customers. With the World Wide Web, online travel sites started displacing travel agencies, as customers could explore and find deals themselves. Low prices and better control over purchases are a strong attraction for customers and difficult to compete with.

When a product or service becomes a commodity, it is easier to standardize it and offer it over the web. This puts power in the hands of the customers. Customers also like uniqueness and don't always choose the standard commoditized product or service. In an earlier time, we would have hired more people to help with the customization. However, now we have a new technology—AI—that can help with that.

Like travel agencies, insurance companies with their vested agent model are at risk. The sale and service of simple products like auto insurance can be done by automated systems, and the sale and service of complex products like life and health insurance can be done with the help of AI systems. Agents will have to invest in enhancing a different set of complementary skills, such as building deeper relationships with customers and empathizing with them in cases of loss.

New, nimbler companies with AI-based business models will threaten the incumbents. AI technologies will give rise to new business models. A company may have the best employees, but if the underlying business model is flawed, the company stands no chance of survival.

As another example, consider typewriters, which have virtually disappeared. Even if you hire the best salespeople to sell typewriters, you will not succeed. That's why the business model is an important element to consider in evaluating an ecosystem.

AI is driving change in business. The ingredients of AI—availability of large amounts of data (or big data), high computing power in the form of GPUs (graphical processing units) and TPUs (tensor processing units), and advanced machine learning algorithms—make it easier for businesses to change and transform themselves. Cloud and technology vendors are offering AI expertise in the form of services that businesses can leverage in their transformation. All the components to enable successful digital transformation are falling into place. This is why the time for AI is now!

6. A Peek into the Future Organization

If you agree that the business ecosystem is going to be disrupted, what will that disruption look like? What role will your organization play in that space?

Your Company's Role

If we think that Google and Amazon are revolutionary companies, I'm sure that we'll be surprised at the kinds of business models that will emerge in a few more years.

Your organization does not exist in isolation. As we have discussed, it exists in an ecosystem with elements such as government regulations, competitors, customers, partners, and so forth. If the enterprise finds its "right" place in this ecosystem, doing the "right" things, then it can thrive.

I'll introduce a new term that embodies the environment in which organizations can find that right place: *hyperscale.* A hyperscale ecosystem is the new ecosystem where organizations interact with one another to provide customer experiences.[18] In this ecosystem, organizations of all sizes can participate. No single organization will provide the "end-to-end" experience for the customer. In such an ecosystem, sometimes organizations collaborate and other times the same ones compete. This has been termed *coopetition* to describe "cooperative competition."

In the digital world of tomorrow, customers will expect the services provided by companies to revolve around them. When self-driving smartcars become a reality, here's one set of interactions that's

---

[18] Michael Chui and James Manyika, "Competition at the Digital Edge: 'Hyperscale' Businesses," *McKinsey & Company*, accessed December 8, 2016, http://www.mckinsey.com/industries/high-tech/our-insights/competition-at-the-digital-edge-hyperscale-businesses.

possible:

Lisa leaves work and walks out of the building. Her car starts itself and comes to the door to pick her up. She hops in, and twenty minutes before she reaches her home, the car sends instructions to adjust the thermostat and turn on the oven. One minute before she enters her house, the music system turns on, playing what she likes. Since Lisa calls her mom every other day on the way home from work, that pattern is learned, and the car asks her if she'd like to call her mom.

The possibilities are endless. The critical thing is that different companies provide different services that are brought together in the context of the customer, Lisa. All services revolve around Lisa, and the companies offering the various services have to collaborate to create the desired experience for her. Your company will probably play only a small role in such an ecosystem of collaborating and competing companies.

The challenge for architects of transformation is to design and deploy services in such a way that they can be combined and reconfigured dynamically with services offered by other organizations to provide uniquely tailored experiences for customers like Lisa.

The following figure illustrates this concept. The ovals represent different companies in the ecosystem, and the size of each oval represents the size of a company relative to others in the ecosystem. Each company may offer different services to complete the end-to-end experience of a customer. Each customer could potentially have a different set and sequence of interactions with several companies, leading to a highly personalized experience.

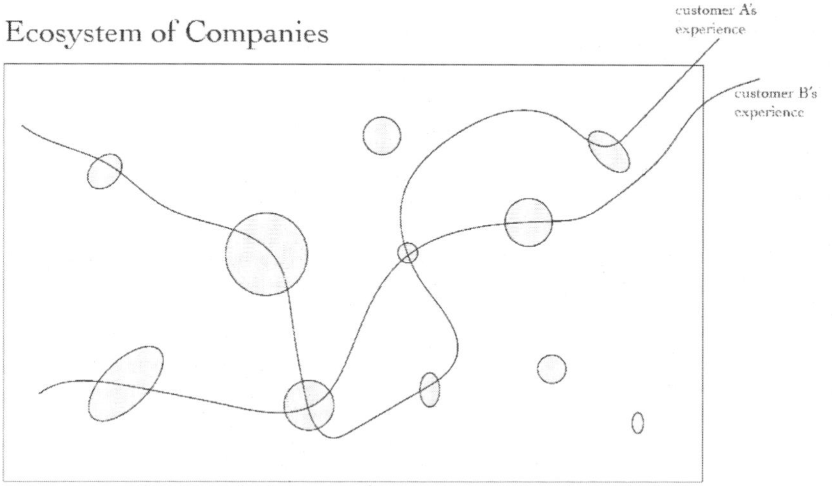

FIGURE 6-1: Ecosystem of companies working with one another

How does this impact your company and, more specifically, your role? Future ecosystems will be large, and it is unlikely that your company will have a dominant role across the whole ecosystem. The company will have to establish partnerships with other companies that provide complementary expertise. Depending upon what part your company chooses to play in this space, your own role may be enhanced or diminished.

Let's say that you work for an insurance company as an actuary whose job is to calculate the customer's risk using advanced mathematical and statistical methods. Today, rating a customer's risk is a critical function. This process requires collecting data about the customer and the object (such as a car) that they are trying to insure. The more data you have, the better you can evaluate the risk. If another company is better at gathering data and evaluating the risk, your company may decide to outsource that function to them and focus on acquisition and customers instead. In this case, even though you have deep knowledge and expertise in evaluating risk, your skills are not needed anymore at your company. In this scenario you would have to either move to a company that can use your skills or learn new skills. Moving to a company that specializes in rating might not be an ideal option either, because risk rating may be automated by machine learning. I'll explore some aspects of automation in the next section.

Autonomy Is the Next Frontier, Beyond Automation

For the past few years, technology has introduced automation to the workplace. This is where machines are programmed to do tasks that previously used to be done by humans. To automate work, we outline the discrete steps that make up the work, then figure out if a combination of hardware and software can do the work or parts of it.

Take the example of people applying for auto loans. They fill out an application providing personal details such as where they live and yearly income, requesting a specific amount. In earlier days, a person evaluated these factors manually based on a set of criteria, and the loan was granted or denied with an interest rate proportional to the applicant's risk of defaulting. The factors affecting the loan repayment and the rules to apply were well understood.

Eventually the whole process was automated with software by codifying the rules. If you knew the input values for the factors, you could follow the logic to get the answer of acceptance or denial. The software was able to do the job faster and without any errors. This put people who handled loan applications out of a job.

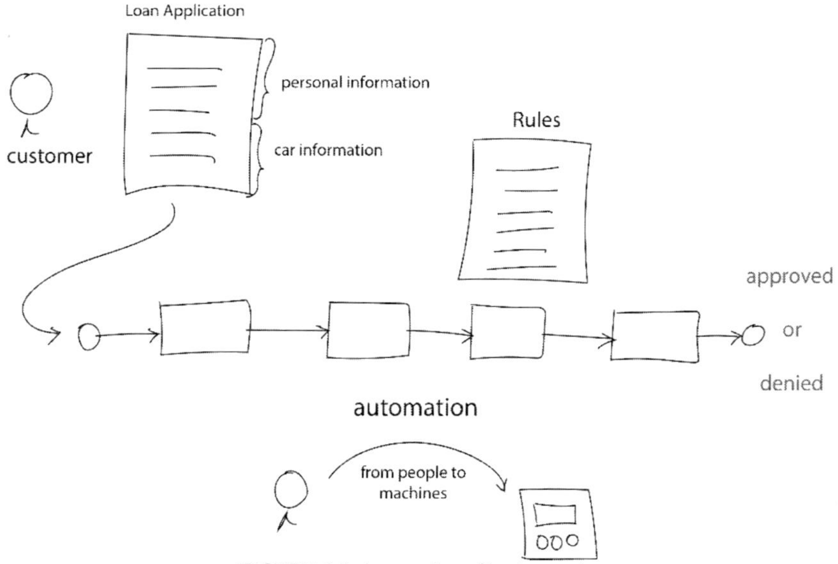

FIGURE 6-2: Automation of business rules

Now let's take automation a step further to autonomy. Autonomy refers to something that requires independent decisions such as making judgment calls. Say a crowd gathers for a peaceful protest, but gradually some people get belligerent. Initial pockets of such disturbances will not affect the overall attitude of the crowd. However, if more and more people start to get violent, the police will make a judgment call. There is not a single "tipping point" at which the protest goes from a peaceful one to a violent one. Knowing when to intervene cannot be easily codified. Unlike the previous case of automation, even if all the factors were the same in two different peaceful protests, the point at which each becomes violent could be different. The ability to make the call is autonomy.

AI operates well in this space of autonomy and is able to make decisions that can assist human decision making. In the above example, an AI system may be able to consume large amounts of previous data about protests, both peaceful and violent, and then notify human decision makers when they have to be concerned. It democratizes the knowledge about protests so a rookie is in as good a position as an expert because the AI system has encoded lots of previous knowledge and makes it available to benefit anyone.

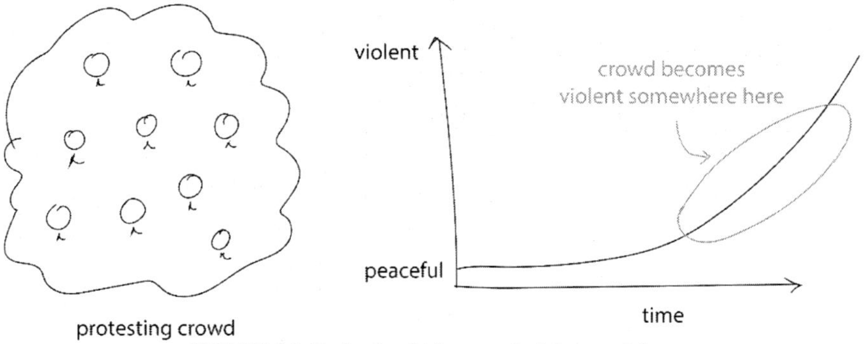

FIGURE 6-3: Region in which a crowd might turn violent

AI Comes into the Picture

Through breakthroughs in the broad field of AI, we are moving from a paradigm of software programming to machine learning. In software programming, computer language is used to tell the computer how to respond. In machine learning, data is fed into the computer so it can detect the underlying patterns and relationships in the data. The computer is still programmed, but the program is not a set of instructions; rather, it gives the machine a specific model, and the model is then populated by the data. If the input data changes, the model values change and therefore the results change.

The programming paradigm is driven by logic, while the machine learning paradigm is driven by data. For the former, we need to understand how the system works to codify it. For the latter, we need to have a considerable amount of data to train the machine. The former is computational and the latter is cognitive. Traditionally, computers have been good at computation while humans have excelled in cognitive tasks. For example, adding up a million numbers is easy for computers and difficult for humans. On the other hand, recognizing objects in a complex environment has been difficult for computers and easy for humans. These complementary strengths have provided the best of both worlds in computer-human collaboration.

With the new paradigm of data-driven models, the line of demarcation on what computers are good at and what humans are good at is blurring, and computers are getting more cognitive abilities. They now can recognize faces, understand natural language and respond, translate between multiple languages, recognize objects in constrained environments, and scan radiography images for tumors, among other things.

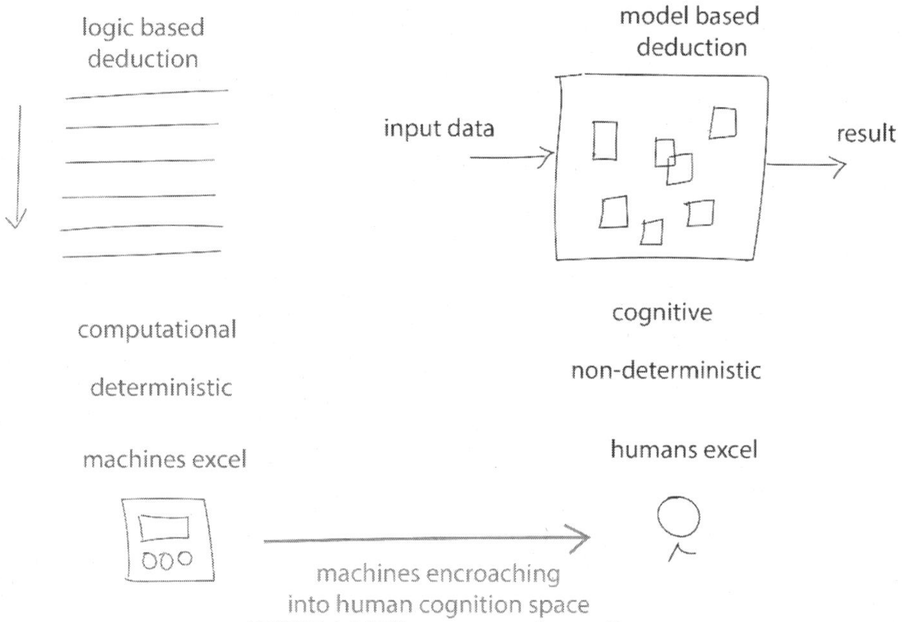

FIGURE 6-4: Different programming paradigms

From Computation to Cognition

Essentially, if computers get enough cognitive abilities, they can do more of what the human mind can do and, in many cases, do it even better. They can make decisions objectively. This will help reduce biases and corruption. Computers also don't get tired, unlike people. For example, some studies have shown that judges are more lenient after lunch.[19] With computers, you don't get this bias. As computers take on cognitive tasks, the daily life of ordinary humans will be enhanced, removing vagaries and idiosyncrasies.

Recent growth in this area has been fueled by the availability of large volumes of data (for example, many people have taken pictures and posted them on the internet, which makes it possible for face recognition algorithms to be developed), higher computing power (as

---

[19] Michael Haederle, "Judges' Decisions More Lenient After Lunch," *Pacific Standard,* April 13, 2011, https://psmag.com/economics/judges-decisions-more-lenient-after-lunch-30179.

dictated by Moore's Law, computing power has approximately doubled every eighteen months), and newer algorithms (statistical models have given way to more complex deep-learning networks). As we move towards what's referred to as artificial general intelligence, we will need some drivers like these to propel us forward, but nobody knows just what those drivers will be.

Are You Prepared?

The question is, are you prepared for this shift? Do you know how it will impact your work? Will your role change or even be eliminated?

Even if you are not a software programmer, your job will change. You may be an executive, a manager, an analyst, an architect, a business professional, or anyone else whose job is to understand the business or parts of it. You have to add data-based thinking into your repertoire of skills, in addition to logic or procedural-based thinking. For example, if you are in marketing, you can't simplistically segment customers based on attributes that you think are important; rather, you have to think about how all the data you have on your customers—such as their purchase and interaction history, their social media interactions, their views on global issues, etc.—are related to the products or services your business offers.

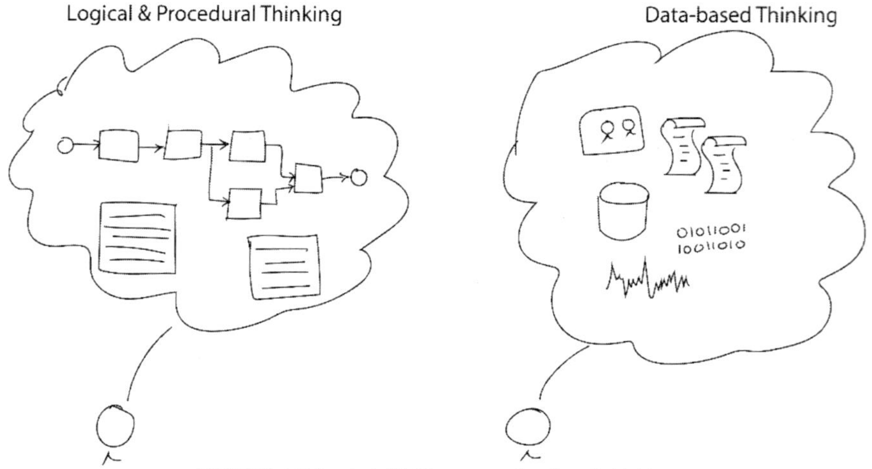

FIGURE 6-5: Logical thinking versus data-based thinking

Almost all jobs will change. The question is how you are going to respond.

7. A Story of Change

Let's conclude Part I with a real story of change and the lessons we can take away from it.

The Kodak Story

In 1975 when Steve Sasson, an engineer at Kodak, invented the first digital camera and told his management about it, they flippantly said, "That's cute—but don't tell anyone."

However, Kodak commissioned a study on how digital cameras could affect its market share. That study not only predicted the dominance of digital photography, but also predicted that Kodak had ten years to adapt to that change. Unfortunately, in those ten years, Kodak did little to adjust.

Prior to this, George Eastman, the company's founder, had made strategic decisions at least twice that steered the company to new profitability. One was to move away from the profitable dry-plate business to film, and the other was the move from the profitable black-and-white film to color, even though in both cases the newer products were inferior to the older ones at the time of the transition.

But at the beginning of the digital era, the company was afraid that digital cameras would cannibalize its film business and so refused to act, though it continued to improve the digital camera technology in its research lab. In 1986, Kodak even developed the first megapixel camera, a predicted tipping point in the digital camera business.

In 1989, when CEO Colby Chandler retired, the board of directors had the opportunity to pick as his replacement between a conservative, Kay Whitmore, and an ardent digital supporter, Phil Samper. The board went with Whitmore, who said that he'd make sure Kodak stayed close to its core business in film and photographic chemicals. After three years of the company spiraling downward, the board fired him.

Kodak considered digital photography as its archenemy and fought it. In January 2012, the much-revered, 131-year-old company filed for bankruptcy. Tens of thousands of jobs were lost in the years leading up to the bankruptcy, and more layoffs followed.

If you had been an employee of Kodak around 2012, you would have had to consider the context of the company for your own professional future. Would the company survive? Would you have a job? If not, what new skills would you have to develop to find a new job?

Vince Barabba, Kodak's head of marketing intelligence who headed the study mentioned above, argues in his book *The Decision Loom*[20] that four things are necessary for an organization to recognize and react appropriately to change.

An organization should:

(1) Have a mindset that is open to change.

(2) Think and act holistically.

(3) Adapt the business design to changing conditions.

(4) Make decisions interactively using a wide variety of methods.

Like Kodak, your company's reaction to the technological advancements in AI may be the defining moment that could change you and your organization. My intent is to help you to think holistically, to identify the change you see coming and identify the skills you need to improve or acquire, and to continuously evaluate your ecosystem so you can make good decisions. In turn, what I need from you is a mindset that is open to change.

Why do I say that your response to AI may be a defining moment?

---

[20] Vincent Barabba, *The Decision Loom: A Design or Interactive Decision-Making in Organizations* (Devon, UK: Triarchy Press Ltd, 2011).

For the first time in U.S. history, today's generation will make less money than the previous generation.[21] Technologies will exacerbate the problem for a certain group of people, and the group that is in the crosshairs of AI comprises a majority of white-collar workers.

Strategic adaptation is key. It is easy to look back at Kodak and analyze what they should have done. The question now is, how can we look forward while observing change around us, adapt ourselves, and do so quickly?

What Will Your Future Look Like?

The rate at which the world is changing around you is rising fast. The gross domestic product (GDP) of the world in the last 100 years is roughly equal to the GDP in the world in the last 10,000 years.[22] Predictions are that the progress in the next ten years will be faster than the previous ten. Are you prepared for that future? Is your organization prepared for that future?

Intellectually knowing what that future looks is only ten percent of the battle. Designing and building the capabilities to thrive in that future is the other ninety percent. So how do you do this?

When computers first became prominent across industries and more work was automated, people were afraid that their jobs would disappear. However, what we found was that while many jobs disappeared, new ones were created. The skills required for the new jobs, however, were different, and those who could not adapt or were not prepared lost their place in the working world.

Just like how computers drove the technological revolution, AI will drive the cognitive revolution. We are already seeing advances that give a glimpse of this world. We can control more and more of our

---

[21] "Will Today's Generation Be Poorer than Their Parents?" *Marketplace,* July 14, 2016, http://www.marketplace.org/2016/07/13/world/flat-income.

[22] Nick Bostrom, *Superintelligence: Paths, Dangers, Strategies* (Oxford University Press, 2016, Kindle Edition), p. 3.

environment through our mobile devices. Sensors can be attached to any physical object to either control it or have it monitor the environment. Self-driving cars will soon be transporting us. Data will be generated in increasing abundance and will be analyzed quickly to understand more about a system and react accordingly. Robots will perform surgeries. Machines will get more and more intelligent. Homes will become smarter.

In the context of such an environment, your work location may be different. Your team will be different. You'll need a different set of skills, depending upon the role you play in that future ecosystem. The systems you interact with will be different. In some sense, things will become easier, and in another sense, they will become harder. The future will be the "best of times [and] the worst of times," as Charles Dickens opens the novel *A Tale of Two Cities.* Rephrasing from Dickens, the cognitive revolution will be the best of times, it will be the worst of times, it will be the age of opportunity, it will be the age of despair, it will be the epoch of control, and it will be the epoch of letting go. We'll have everything before us, and we'll have nothing before us, for it will be a complex world in which humankind has to adapt to the vicissitudes of the dynamic ecosystem.

PART II: UNDERSTAND—TOOLS TO MODEL YOUR ECOSYSTEM

In Part I, hopefully I convinced you that change is happening and that it's time for you to adapt. This process is not "once-and-done," but continual throughout your life.

Before we can adapt, we need to understand our ecosystem. We can do that by creating models that represent specific aspects of the ecosystem. For example, the familiar organizational chart of a company is a representation of how the leadership team and departments are organized. To model the ecosystem, you have to be familiar with a set of visual tools that you can use. In part, we'll just explore these modeling tools. Not all of them will make sense now, and most readers can skim through this section to get an understanding of the categories of tools and come back to it later as a reference.

This section is organized by tools that can be used to model ecosystems.

8. Simple Modeling Concepts

There are so many ways to model that I can't cover them all comprehensively in just one book. I will introduce a few ways to model ecosystems, and once you get familiar with these and use them, you will become quite comfortable exploring variations and becoming more creative.

Models can be created for yourself or for others to consume. The most important thing to understand is that your model should meet the needs of your audience (also called a consumer), be it yourself or others. If there are different consumers, you may have to create different models for them. However, you should thoroughly understand how those models are connected.

Basic Elements

When you look around your ecosystem, you see many elements. Some of these are tangible and others intangible. Modeling is about representing these elements. As you get familiar with them, you might create a library of such elements that you can reuse.

Two different people might have two different libraries, though there may be some common elements. For example, for a person who needs to understand the railway system in the U.S., a train may be one single element. For a person who is designing trains, the parts of the train may be separate elements. The former is not interested in anything more granular than the train because they are concerned about how the train fits into the bigger picture. On the other hand, the latter wants to understand how all the parts of the train fit together.

Keep It Simple

"I knew it was time to simplify our organization when we started creating acronyms for our acronyms."

FIGURE 8-1: Used with permission

Rephrasing Einstein, a model should be as simple as possible but no simpler. When you model your ecosystem, your intention should be to understand and leverage it to your advantage. To do that, you'll have to capture enough information in it, but not too much. More data for your model is not necessarily a good thing.

Making that judgment is a combination of experience and heuristics. If in doubt, you should err on the side of minimal information, because if you try to err on the other side, you will not know where to stop. Most times, models can be built incrementally.

A model has to be continually maintained to keep it current. After all, we are modeling the ecosystem, which is continuously changing.

Say you are modeling the transportation of explosive goods. It's important to understand the characteristics of the transporting mechanism to avoid the risk of explosions. You want to capture these characteristics in your model because they are critical to understanding the problem space. Perhaps you need a good shock-absorbing system to prevent a bumpy ride; perhaps you need sirens to warn other vehicles that this one is carrying an explosive load; perhaps you need an onboard fire extinguishing mechanism in case of an emergency, etc. These characteristics are important to capture. On the other hand, you may not have to worry about things like whether the vehicle has a GPS or whether the dashboard is designed ergonomically. It's not that those features are unimportant; it's just that they are not relevant for your context. They might be relevant in a different context for a different purpose.

Understanding the Consumer

Models are created for consumers: yourself or others. Since the main theme of this book is to help you adapt to the future, you are the consumer. However, there are some consumer-centered principles in model design that apply no matter who the consumer is:

- *Simple:* Designed to the consumer's needs—as simple as possible but no simpler. Aim for clarity.
- *Reflects reality:* Show reality, whether it is about the current ecosystem or a possible future ecosystem.
- *Different perspectives:* You may need separate models for different perspectives, and sometimes more than one model for a particular perspective.
- *Multiple models:* Learn to use more and more concepts. There is more than one way to model the same thing.
- *Focus on content:* Focus on the content, not on creating pretty pictures.
- *Build a library:* Develop a list of "best models" and "best visuals" to build your library of tools.
- *Right level of detail:* Capture only the level of detail you need for your analysis.
- *Modularity:* If your model is too big, try to group things in a logical fashion. If the parts of your model are modular, you can easily replace one part without affecting the others.

- *Integration:* The various parts of your model will connect. Make sure that the integration across the parts is clear.

- *Notation:* Use notation and notes to help you read your models, much like a legend on a map.

- *Building as you go:* You don't have to complete the full model in one shot. Take an incremental approach and add to the model as you learn more about the ecosystem.

- *Time-stamp:* Some models need a timeframe associated with them. For example, you may construct different models to capture the current, five-year-future, and twenty-year-future states.

Labeling Elements and Relationships

There are two types of elements around us—tangibles and intangibles (usually these can be identified with nouns). Some of these elements are connected to one another. Say you represent tangibles with rectangles, intangibles with ovals, and the connections between them as lines. Then you can draw a picture of rectangles, ovals, and lines. In addition, you can use text to annotate parts of the model, and you can make the lines directional. Here's the illustration of the notation followed by an example that uses that notation.

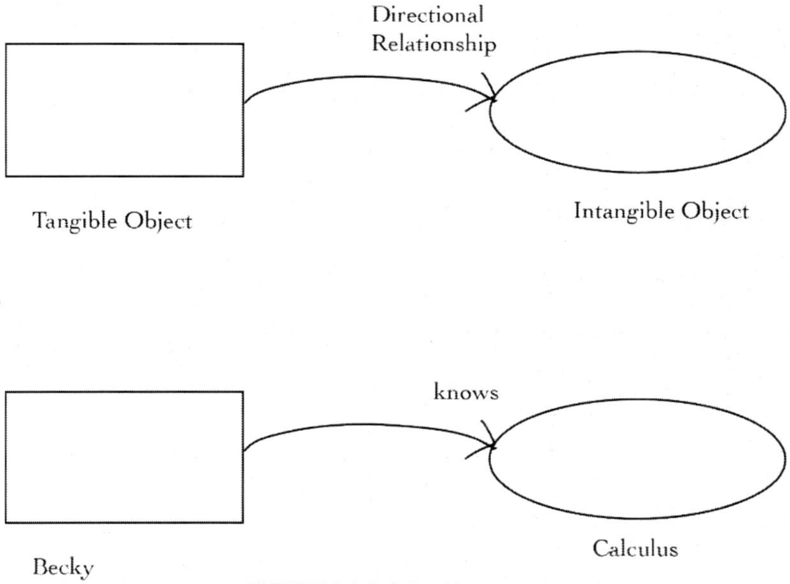

FIGURE 8-2: Relationship concept

What the model says here is, "Becky knows calculus." Let's make it a little better. Even though humans are tangibles, since you model them a lot, you may want to give them their own symbol—something like a stick figure.

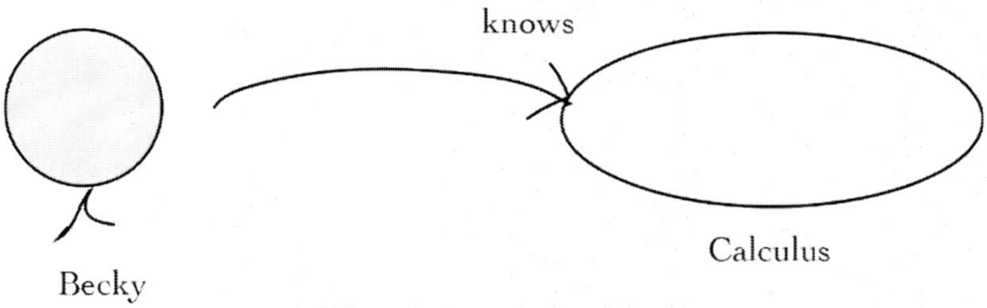

FIGURE 8-3: Human in the relationship

Terms and Models

Business terms are critical to understanding the ecosystem. As you come across familiar or unfamiliar terms, you will want to capture them along with a brief definition or description. Business terms do not exist in isolation; rather, many are related to one another. A business-term model can show such relationships.

For example, a customer may be assigned an agent, and the customer may have purchased some products through the agent and other products directly through the company. We can model this if needed, and it may look something like this:

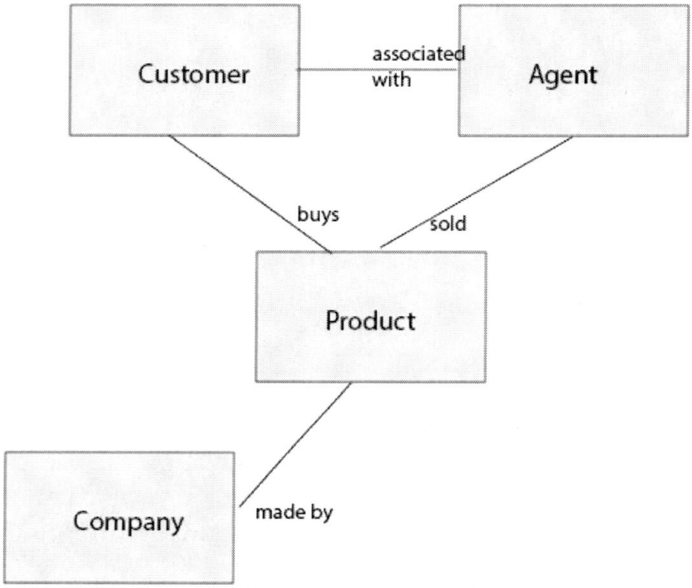

FIGURE 8-4: Terms and models

Syntactic versus Semantic Representations

Syntactic models show literal things. Semantic models express meaning.

Let's first consider syntactic models. Such models convey the structural relationship between parts—much like what an object itself would look like. An example of this kind of model would be the floor plan of an apartment. In this case, you can imagine yourself walking through the apartment and you'd know where the walls are and where doors lead to.

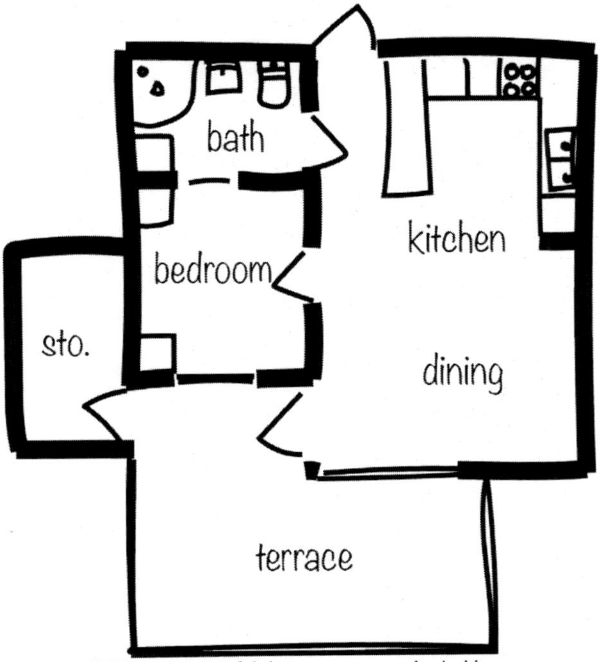

FIGURE 8-5: Model that represents a physical layout

Unlike syntactic models, semantic models convey meaning among parts, such as the material that each part of a house is made of. This type of model could be a "tree" with the whole house as the root node, and the parts of it as children of that node. Each part, such as a room node, can be further split into child nodes that show the walls, doors, etc. Each leaf node in this tree can contain the material that that part is made of. Using this model, you can illustrate that the doors are made of wood and the walls of concrete.

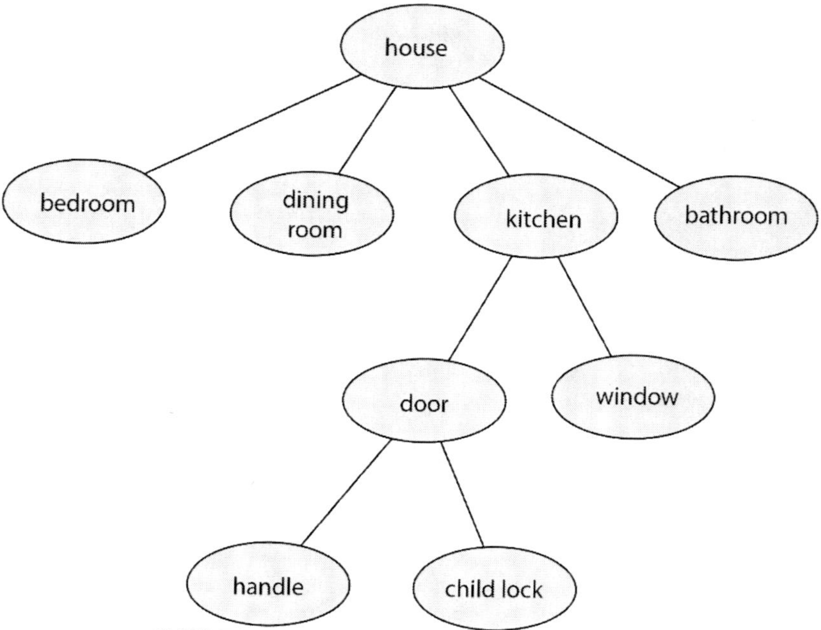

FIGURE 8-6: Model that represents components of a house

However, you wouldn't be able to use this model to walk through the house as with the previous model. As you can see, each type of representation or model serves a different purpose.

When there are two objects in a model—say, a person and a chair—you can draw the chair and person in any number of ways. For example, your representation can be as simple as this:

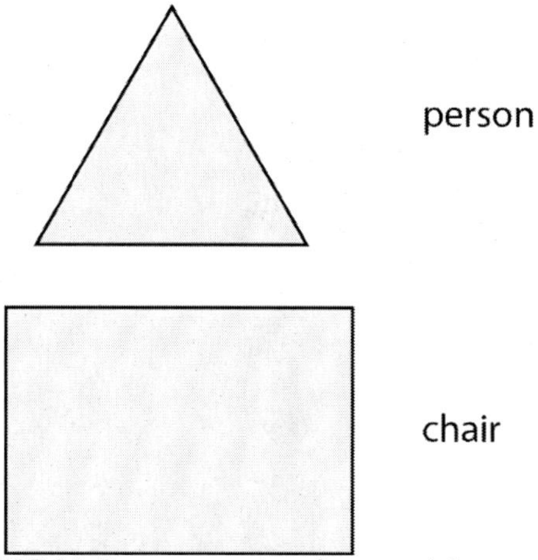

FIGURE 8-7: One representation of a person sitting on a chair

The triangle looks nothing like a person, and the rectangle nothing like a chair—but the semantic meaning of a person sitting on a chair is conveyed. Modeling for our purposes has more to do with semantic notions than literal notions. This abstraction also helps you avoid focusing too much on the likeness of the objects and instead focus on the relationships between them.

As you can imagine, there are many ways to model a person sitting on a chair and this is just one of them. Four other visual ways that communicate this concept are shown in the variations below:

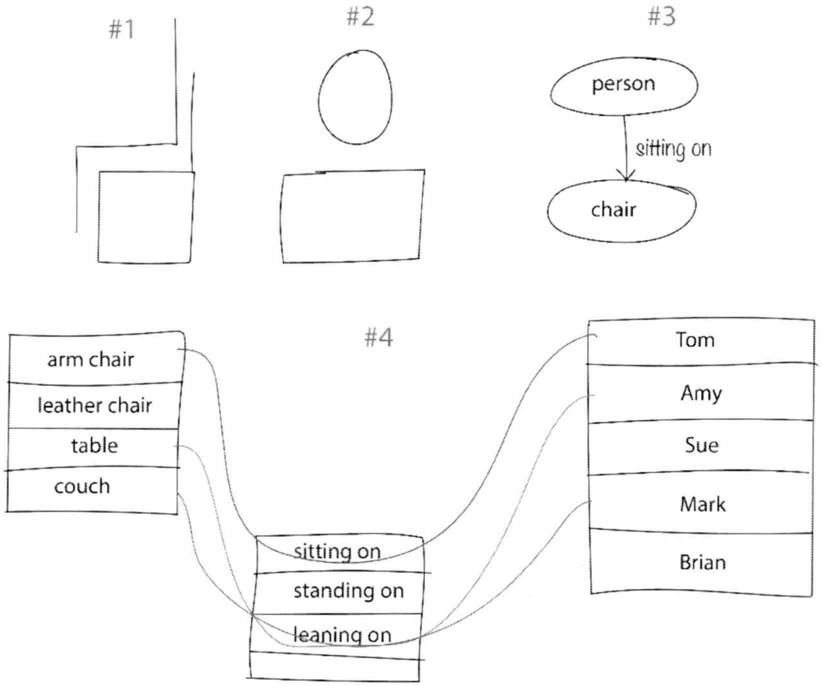

FIGURE 8-8: Other representations of a person sitting on a chair

Which model you create depends on what you want to understand about the ecosystem. In the more complex variation shown as #4, we could create a representation across multiple people and multiple pieces of furniture to depict different relationships of different people with the furniture. That complex model implies that Tom is sitting on an arm chair, while Amy is leaning on a table, and Mark is leaning on a couch.

Depicting People

In many of my models, people are the focus and should be treated specially. That's why they get their own special icon that looks this:

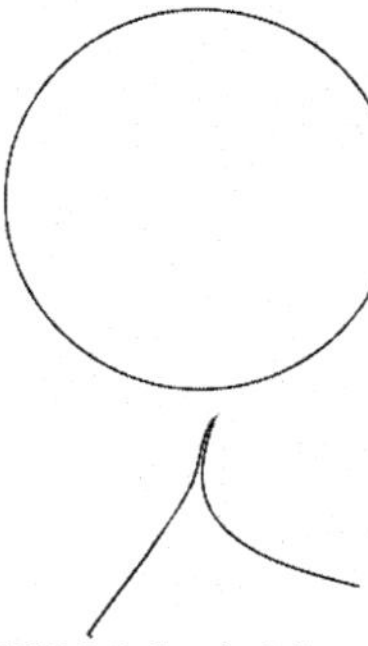

FIGURE 8-9: Symbol for a human

This, of course, is my way of representing people. If you are a better artist, you can change that icon and get as creative as you wish. The point, however, is not to focus on the realism of depicting a person at the expense of losing the information that you are trying to understand or convey. A simple stick figure should do.

In some cases you do want to depict different things about different people. You could choose to do that through color (as we will below when depicting leadership) or by simply adding text.

Sometimes you will want to show individuals, and in some cases a group of people. To be efficient in your visual representation, you should try to stick to the simplest representations, yet be distinctive. In other words, you don't want the whole picture to be filled with rectangles. That will make it too mundane and, more importantly, unreadable.

Modeling the Abstract

We don't always model physical things. For example, we could model abstract things like culture, customer sentiment, or leadership qualities.

For example, we know that some people are great leaders. What makes them so great? Models can help us think deeply about this question.

Research about effective leadership points to qualities such as communication, confidence, honesty, the ability to delegate, inspirational capacity, creativity, intuition, approach to problem solving, attitude, and drive. I've chosen to use ovals to build a primitive mechanism to represent these intangible qualities. How can we compare such leadership qualities, say between Tim and Sandy?

We could draw something like this, where each oval represents a particular attribute:

FIGURE 8-10: Comparing attributes of two people

This would be a subjective representation, but you can still use it for your point of view to be able to understand your ecosystem better. As you learn more, you can refine your own model.

Of course, this is only one way to model the many human attributes. You can get as creative as you want. Remember, this is your model, and it should first make sense to you.

You could model it as a table, with values, say, in the range of 1 to 5.

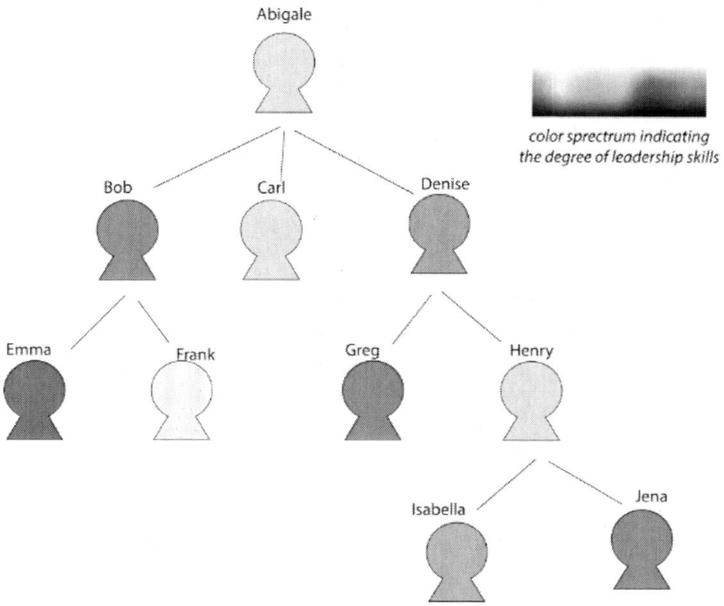

FIGURE 8-11: More information than just an organizational chart

Or you could model it with color, comparing different leaders, where they fall on the organizational chart, and how effective each one is.

	Communication	Confidence	Honesty	Delegation	Etc.
Sandy	3	5	1	0	
Tim	5	2	1	2	

TABLE 8-1

These measures are indeed subjective. While Randy thinks that Sandra is a great leader, Tom may think that she is not such a great leader. Conceptual models can only represent what we think we know. They cannot come up with the magic objective answer.

Similarly, things like culture, software applications, politics, organizational structures, ideas, and innovation can also be modeled. Just like an artist who can paint the picture any way they want, you too have the creative freedom to represent things in the way you want. There is no standard for that, nor should there be.

Distances and Proximities

In modeling, sometimes it is important to represent relative distance, and other times not. Maps usually preserve relative distance between places because we want to get a sense for how the places on the map are distributed relative to one another. This also helps us understand how long it would take to drive from one town to another. Looking at a map, we can guess that Bloomington, Illinois is about halfway between St. Louis and Chicago.

Sometimes you might want to know the relative population of cities, in which case you can draw circles around the cities that show relative population sizes. They have no relation to the boundaries of the cities themselves.

Space and Time Models

How do you capture space and time? A map captures space and shows the relative distance between places. However, you can add more features to the map so it does not necessarily only represent distances, but provides other information.

The following subway map of London[23] is a good example of how a map has been extended to suit its audience—travelers. A rider needs to know the stations along the way, the train (which is color coded), and some sense of the relative distance between stations. The layout of the subway map is typically along vertical, horizontal and diagonal axes, even though the actual subway could have twists and turns in its path. This is because riders do not care about the actual

---

[23] "London Underground Overground DLR Crossrail Map," *Transport for London,* licensed under Creative Commons, accessed January 2, 2019, https://commons.wikimedia.org/wiki/File:London_Underground_Overground_DLR_Crossrail_map.svg.

path, but they do care to know where to get on and where to get off, the fare, and similar information.

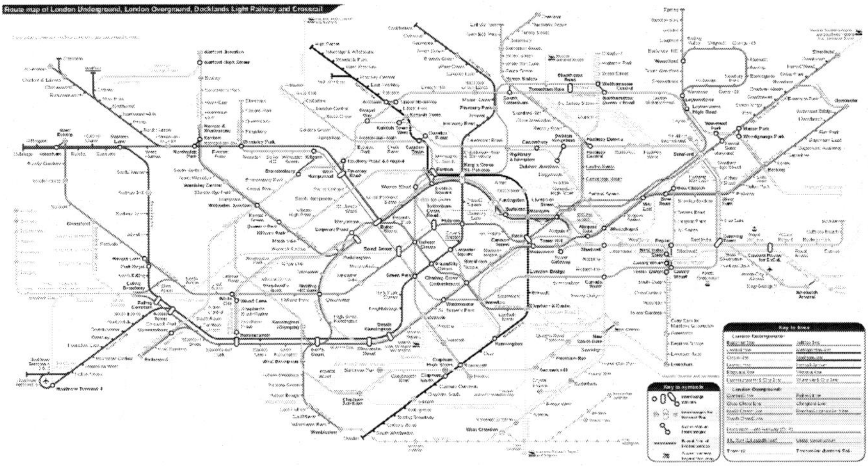

FIGURE 8-12: London subway map

To understand how to capture time, consider the familiar example of a strategic roadmap. The primary intent of a roadmap is to convey information about the progress of work through time. The roadmap will capture information about project start times, durations, milestones, and end times.

Modeling Networks

A network is a common representation that typically illustrates how different elements connect with one another. Social network structures are examples of this.

Below is a network diagram that shows how different computers' peripherals are connected to one another.

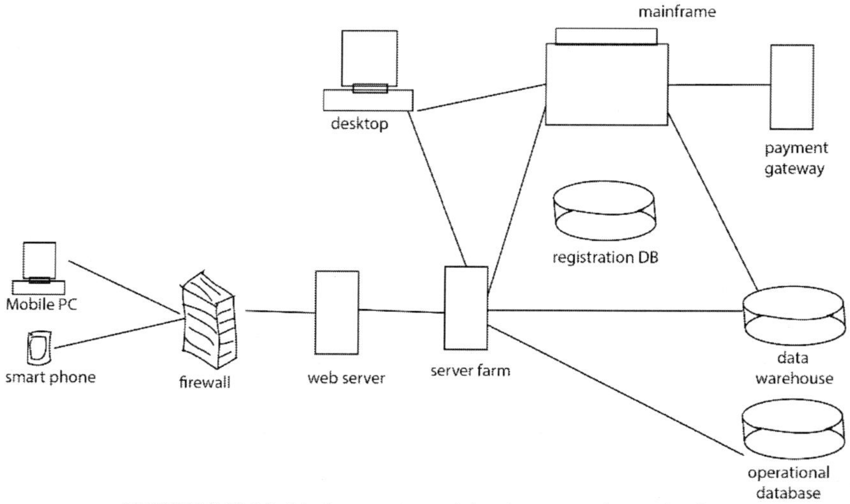

FIGURE 8-13: Model of computing peripherals connected to each other

Tables

A table is a very common model. Whenever you are using a spreadsheet to capture data, you are likely using a model where the data is organized into rows and columns. Each row in the table represents a different entry (also called an instance), and each column represents the value for a particular attribute.

The students of a class can be listed on a table, for example. Their grades in each subject can be listed along the columns.

Student	History	Math	Science	English	PE
Sam Mayden	A	B	A	A	B
Tom Swinger	C	A	B	B	C
Paula Welch	A	C	C	D	A

Julie Roberts	A	B	B	A	A

TABLE 8-2

A table shows two-dimensional data. What if you wanted to show three-dimensional data? Then you can think of the table as extending into one more dimension, as if we have multiple tables stacked together.

Modeling data in even higher dimensional space is possible, although that is much more difficult to visualize. The math used to compute the distance between two points in a high-dimensional space is simply an extended version of the calculation in a two-dimensional space. So even though we can't visualize the higher dimensional space, we can still apply math to calculate, for example, a similarity measure. We will not get into this complexity, other than providing a reference.[24]

Overlaps and Variations

How do you show the differences and similarities between two elements? You can use Venn diagrams, which are simple circles drawn to represent things like size and overlaps.

From the picture below, once you identify the circles that represent the employees, managers, and males, you can make a few inferences.

---

[24] Raj Ramesh, "Don't Leave Your Data Scientist Alone!" *LinkedIn Pulse,* November 17, 2016, https://www.linkedin.com/pulse/dont-leave-your-data-scientist-alone-raj-ramesh-ph-d-.

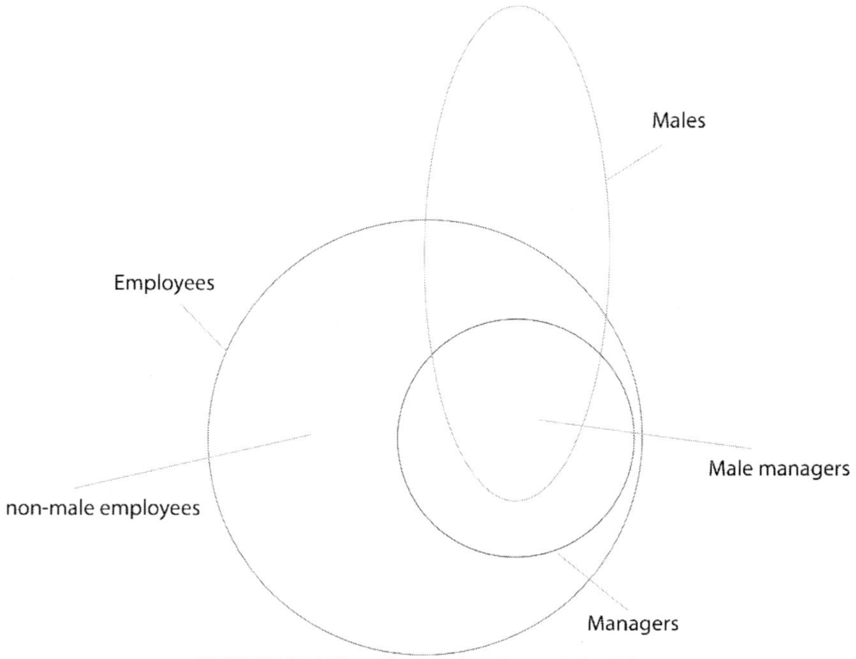

FIGURE 8-14: Venn diagram that shows relationships

For example, you know that all managers are employees, some managers are male, some males are not employees, and so on. This kind of representation is useful to understand roles or possibly products in an organization. If, say, the customer is not able to clearly see in their mind what products serve what needs, they may get confused about the offerings. To avoid this kind of confusion, Steve Jobs simplified Apple's product offerings to better meet customer needs (I will discuss this in more detail later).

Summary

We've explored different types of the most common models that you can use to represent a variety of concepts. Certain models may have applications in specific situations, but at the same time it's dangerous to be prescriptive with them. Experiment with them and use one that is appropriate for you in the system you are trying to understand.

9. Complex Modeling Concepts

While it's ideal in many situations to use simple models, in some situations we have to capture more complexity. In this chapter I'll share models that are a little more complicated.

Illustrating Customer Interactions or Complex Journeys

A customer or user interacts with your company through channels such as web, mobile, call center, or face-to-face interaction. This concept can be modeled as shown below:

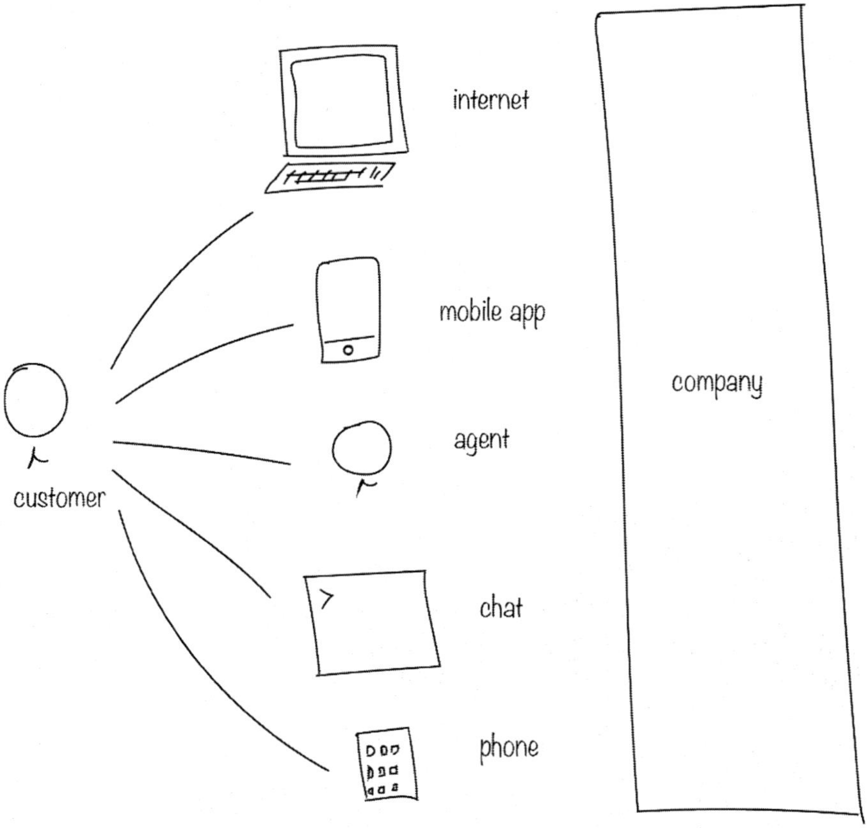

FIGURE 9-1: Channels to interact with the customer

There are others ways to illustrate these interactions, such as user experience maps, many examples of which you may find on the web.[25]

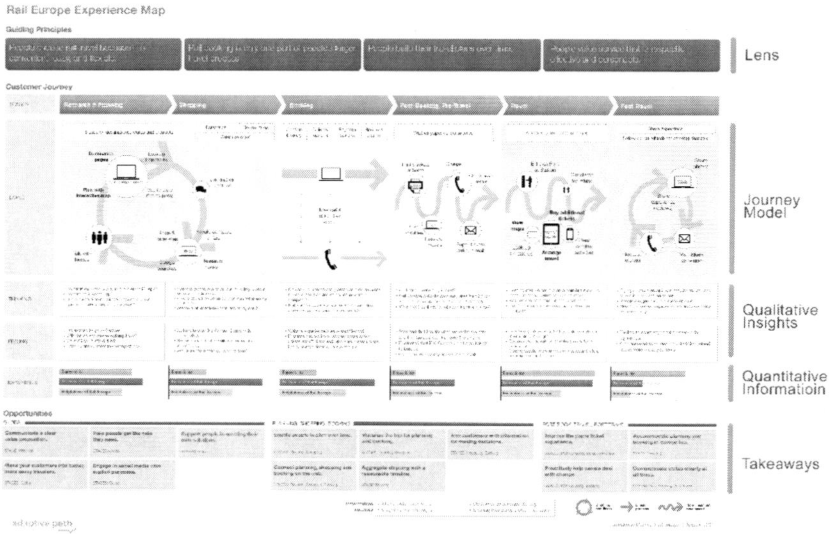

FIG

URE 9-2: Experience map

Services

While "services" sounds a little technical, each of us experiences them every day. When you go to a restaurant, you get service. When you mail a package at the post office, you get service. When you check into a hotel, you get service. In fact, service is so common that often we need to model it.

Let's take an example of hailing a cab. We can represent that visually as I do below:

---

25 "The Anatomy of an Experience Map," *Adaptive Path,* licensed under Creative Commons, accessed January 2, 2019, https://www.adaptivepath.org/ideas/the-anatomy-of-an-experience-map/.

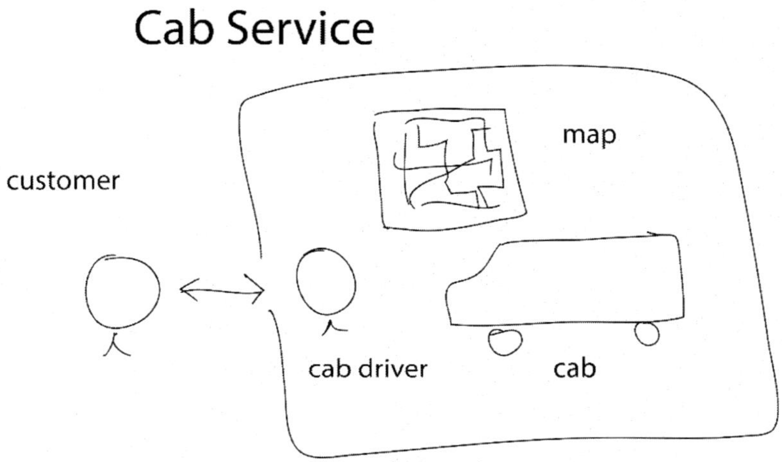

FIGURE 9-3: Model for a cab service

Here, you talk to the cab driver about getting a ride. The cab driver uses a car and a map to get you to the right place. You don't care about those tools (for the most part) or where the cab driver fills up with gas. You have a certain expectation of service by the cab driver to take you to the place you want to go. The cab driver may use many other things to provide that service—such as a gas station, a repair shop for their repairs, a local government office for getting their license, etc. As far as you are concerned, that's all a "black box." Hence, we can put all that stuff into the box shown in the visual above.

Orchestrating Multiple Services

In the real world, services at many levels of granularity are combined in different ways to offer more complex services. When you travel from one city to another, you take a cab for local transportation to the airport, you take a plane to get you to the other city, you stay in a hotel, and you might to go an amusement park. That interaction with multiple services is shown visually here:

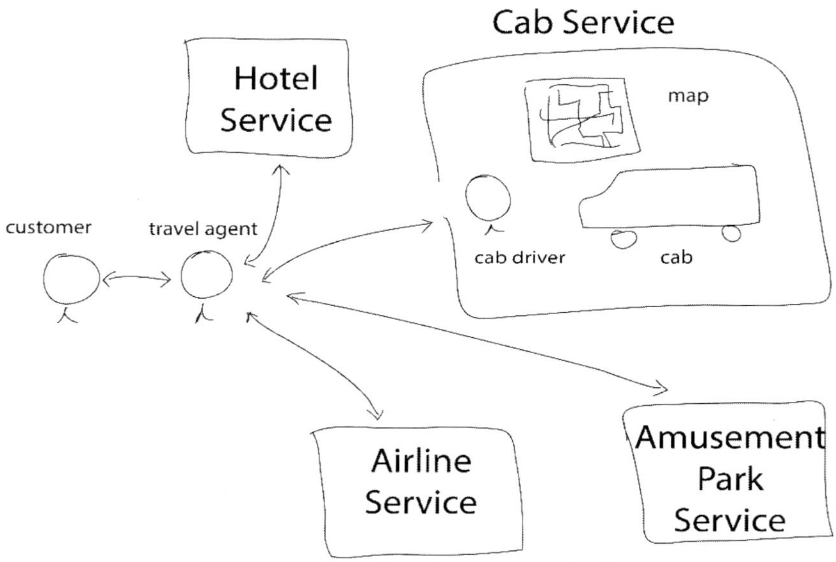

FIGURE 9-4: Model for an integrated set of services

Transformation of State

A model usually represents the ecosystem of interest at a particular point in time. Most ecosystems will change over time, sometimes quite rapidly. However, you may or may not want to know about such changes.

Let's consider the example of a town. Over time, the town changes—with new buildings being constructed and old ones demolished. New roads may be built, people move in, people move out, and so on. However, if you capture every detail about the town, the state changes every second. Lisa, a homeowner, might be in her kitchen at exactly 9:00 a.m., and a few seconds later she might be in the garage. The ecosystem has changed because Lisa's location has changed.

A town planner is not interested in such changes. He is more interested in *major* changes over time, major being defined by the town planner as "significant enough." If, say, the mayor is interested in understanding how the town will change over time as construction projects are completed, then we need to create many snapshots of the model over time at a frequency of, say, every quarter.

This means that we need the concept of a *state* associated with a model. Typically, we create models that reflect the current state, a future state (which may or may not have a defined time horizon), and a few intermediate states. The general principles of modeling apply to any particular state.

FIGURE 9-5: Illustration of state changes over time

The current state model will show the mayor what the town looks like now. The one-year model will show the mayor what the town will look like in one year. The three-year model will show the mayor what the town will look like in three years, and so on. In essence, you have created a representation of what the town will look like at a future point in time.

Process Modeling

Process maps are some of the most common visual models you may come across at your organization. Fundamentally, a process map is a visual representation of the steps required to do something of value. For example, when a customer asks for an insurance quote for their car, the insurance company takes the customer information and goes through a set of steps that includes evaluating the accuracy of the information, authenticating the customer, evaluating the risk, etc. before it provides the quote. These steps can be modeled with a process map.

A process model will look like this. The "lanes" that run horizontally can show the different people or computer systems that play a role in the process. The rectangles show the steps, and the diamonds show decisions that need to be made along the way. There is a starting point and an ending point, as shown by the unfilled circle to the left and the filled one to the right, respectively.

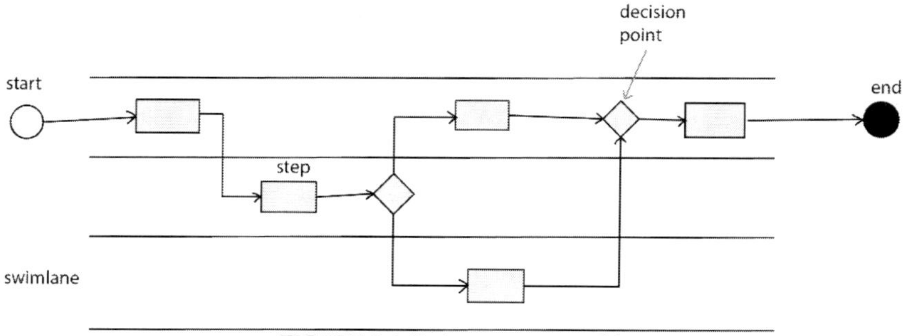

FIGURE 9-6: Business process model

Here's a video that shows many different ways to model a process:

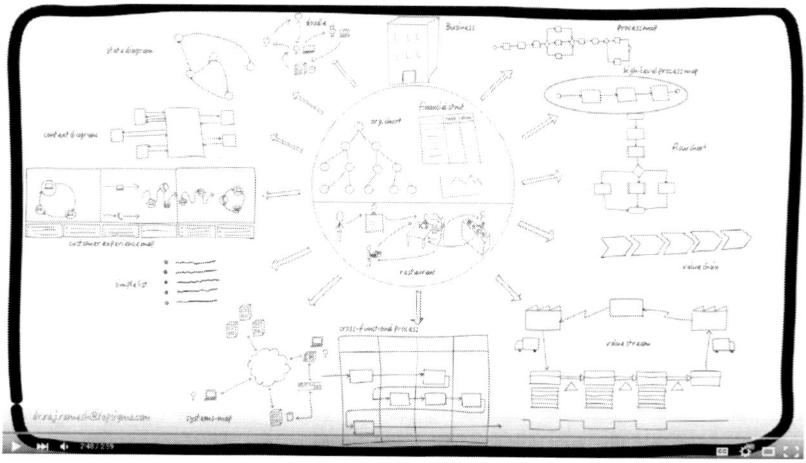

FIGURE 9-7: Video on different ways to model a process

Context Diagram

A context diagram is another useful modeling construct if you want to understand the interactions one element has with many others in the ecosystem. In the real world, there are many elements, and each element interacts with many others. However, if you were to look at all such interactions at the same time, understanding the whole ecosystem could be difficult.

To get around this, you could focus on a single element and try to understand the interactions that element has with its ecosystem. Take, for example, the person taking your order at a fast food service window. Here's the interaction that person will have with other elements in their ecosystem within the context of that order. In the picture below, the person taking your order is placed in the center, and you are the customer.

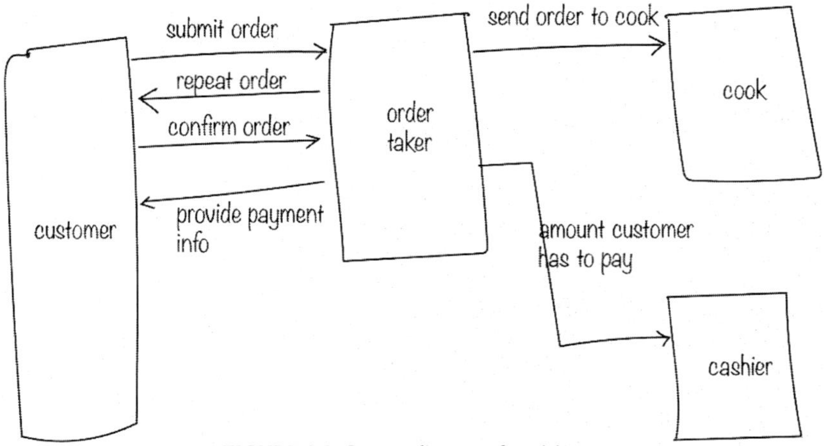

FIGURE 9-8: Context diagram of participants

To create a context diagram, you'll first need to identify the main entity that will be your focus. Then you'll identify all the other entities (such as people or systems) that this entity interacts with. Think through what could happen and draw the visual. Sometimes, it is easier if you think through a particular scenario and draw the lines in sequence as things are exchanged between the entities. You can also number the lines if you want.

Hierarchical Structures or Trees

We come across hierarchical structures, also called "trees," a lot. Examples include how files are organized in your computer using file folders, your company's management structure, and how a country is broken down by states, counties, and towns.

Hierarchical representation is a common and powerful model that can show how the individual components make up the whole. Organizational structures are usually modeled this way to understand reporting relationships. If a system can be broken down into nonoverlapping parts, then you can use a hierarchical model to gradually break down the system into smaller and smaller parts. The great thing about this kind of model is that it is easy to ignore parts that you are not interested in.

Taking the reporting structure below as an example, we can draw what is commonly called an organizational chart that depicts the reporting structure in your company.

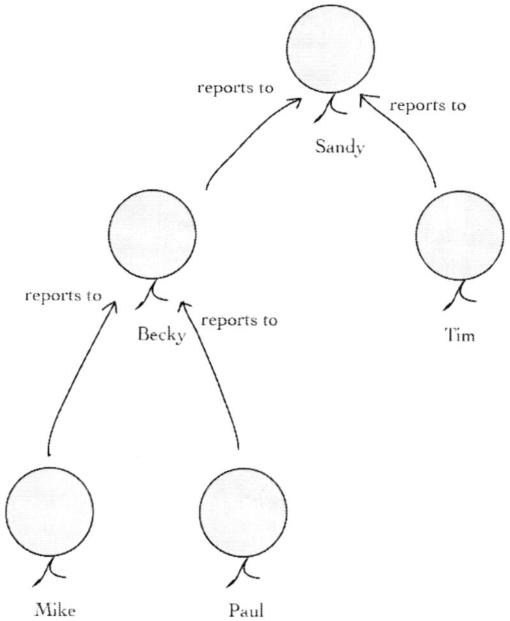

FIGURE 9-9: Reporting structure

Some companies find themselves in a position where very few

decisions get made. They may have too many leaders who don't necessarily agree with one another. That problem becomes painfully obvious in an organizational chart model.

"At one point, I had seventeen vice presidents. That's when I realized it was time to restructure the company and get back to basics."

FIGURE 9-10: Used with permission

Adding Additional Attributes

Now let's say that in addition to the reporting structure, we want to understand how much each person is getting paid. How can we illustrate it visually? First, pay is an abstract concept, so as per our basic notation, it could be represented as an oval. In the picture below, I've added green ovals of various sizes to denote how much each person is paid on a relative scale.

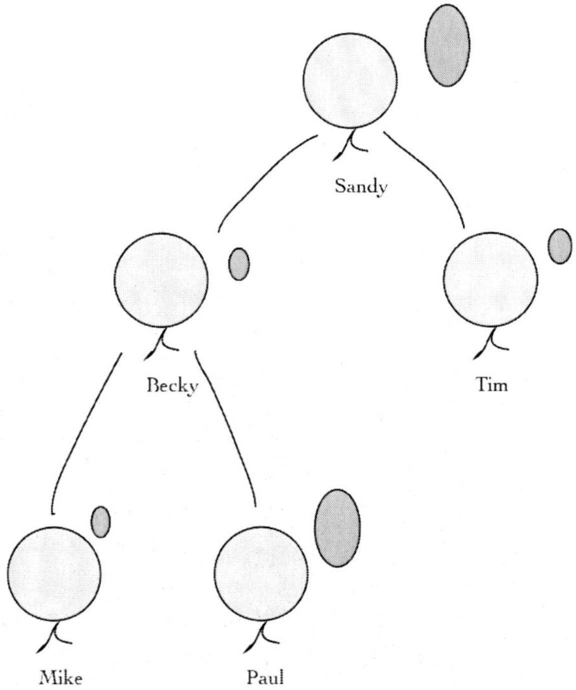

FIGURE 9-11: Enhanced reporting structure

We can tell that even though Paul and Sandy are at different levels of management, their paychecks are about the same.

Just like pay, we can continue to add other attributes that we want to model. The model should be relevant to what we are trying to understand about the ecosystem. Other attributes could be such things as scope of influence, number of people managed, expertise, etc.

Here's another example of a tree (or hierarchy), which calls out the parts that make up a computer.

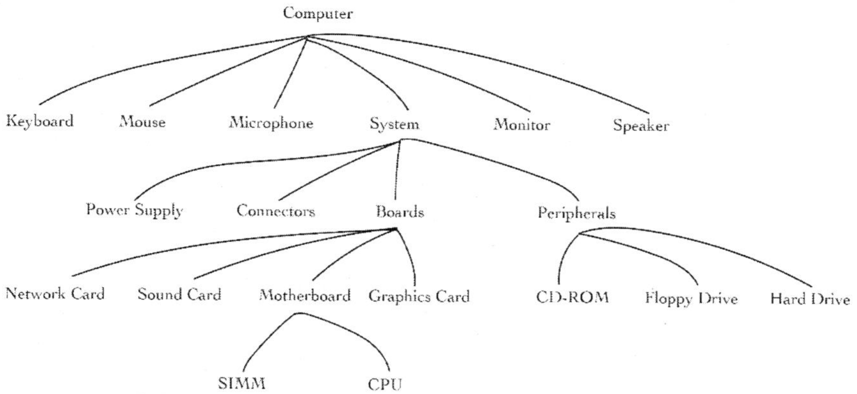

FIGURE 9-12: A hierarchical representation of computer components

When you look at the decomposition of the computer above, you'll see that there are some parts not broken down into greater detail because perhaps we're not interested in them. The CPU is the core of the computer, but if you're a person who is building a computer by putting together all these different parts, you are not be interested in understanding what the CPU itself is made of. All you care about is that it fits in the motherboard that you are going to put it in. This concept of hiding the details within a box is called *encapsulation,* which I will discuss in more detail later.

Logical Decomposition

In the tree structure I discussed above, we take a single element and break it down into parts, and we can continue to do so as we go "deeper and deeper" into the tree.

What if, on the other hand, you want to think about multiple perspectives of the same entity? A good example is how different specialists understand the human body. The human body can be considered from a physiological perspective, from a neurological perspective, from an anatomical perspective, and so on. The same entity is considered from different perspectives—not necessarily broken down into is constituent parts.

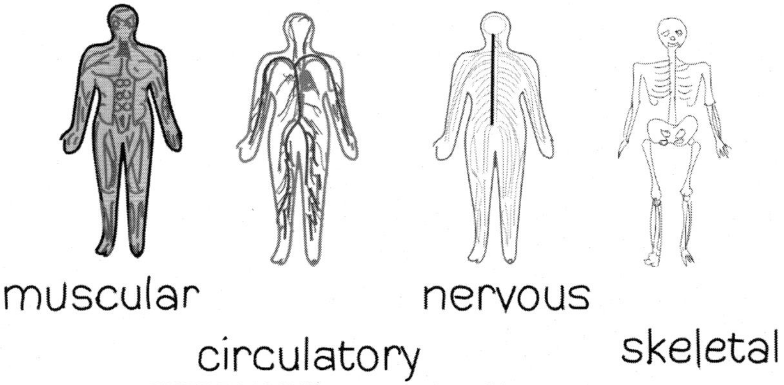

FIGURE 9-13: Different perspectives of the same system

Let's consider some common ways to logically break up a system. One could be a structural decomposition, where different physical parts are considered to be different components. Thinking about your organization, you might mentally break it down into different areas in the company building like the reception area, manufacturing floor, office rooms, cafeteria, and bathrooms. Typically, people who are responsible for reconfiguring physical space think in these terms.

Alternatively, you might logically decompose your organization by function—such as customer call center, finance, HR, engineering, and manufacturing. Typically, people who are responsible for the organizational make-up (such as managers) think in these terms.

Yet another way to logically group components of your organization could be by people's skills and needs. You might accommodate different schedules, disabilities, or tool requirements for the job. Typically, people in the human resources department think in these terms.

Essentially, there is no single way to break up the system, and the way you do it depends on your needs. It may be difficult to standardize the modeling process across an organization because requirements vary. Shown below is the concept that the same system can be broken down into different logical organizations, depending upon your needs.

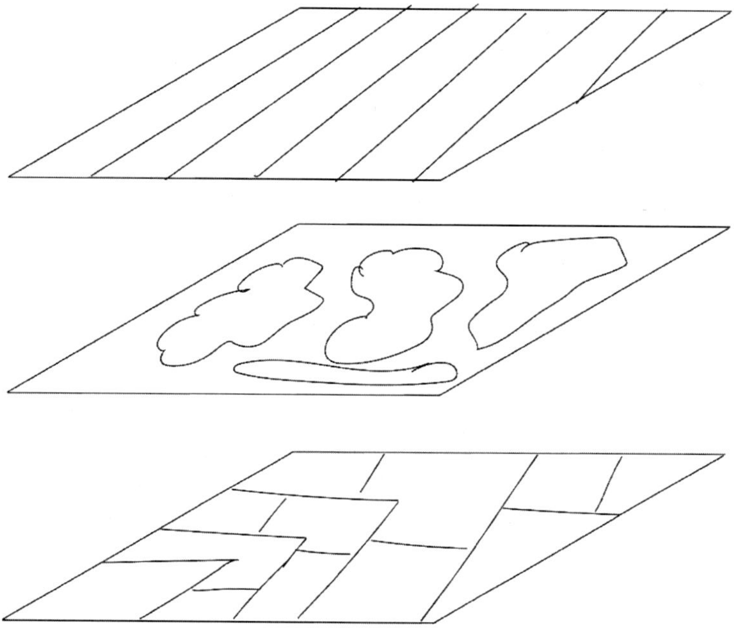

FIGURE 9-14: Different logical views of the same system

Summary

In this chapter we explored more complex models to show you that models can be altered as required to suit your needs. Nothing is sacred about the models discussed. They all can and should be altered to serve your purpose.

10. Desirable Model Properties

There are some properties of models that can make them easier to read and analyze. For example, by being able to "hide" parts of the model that you don't care about, it is easier to analyze it holistically. Otherwise, if you had to always look at the big, detailed picture, then analysis could get complicated.

In the following sections, I will cover some of these properties. You don't have to have all of them in the models you create, but note that some of these can come in handy.

Encapsulation

As you break up a system into logical parts that are relevant to your context, there will be some parts that you know exist but may not care to understand more about. In that case, you'll just encapsulate them in a "black box." By doing this, you'll understand how that box interacts with other parts in your system without necessarily knowing the internals of the box.

A light bulb designer, for example, needs to know how their light bulb will be screwed into the standard socket in the interface, but does not have to worry about the wiring configuration, how electricity is generated and delivered to the bulb, or how it is monitored, even though the light bulb cannot function without those parts of the ecosystem. To the light bulb designer, the rest of the system is encapsulated.

On the other hand, the electrician who is responsible for bringing electricity to the building needs to worry about how to get it there but does not worry about how it's generated or how the light bulb functions.

In some cases, you might be interested in the whole system and need to ensure that the different parts of it are in place and work with one another through well-defined interfaces. In other cases, like the light bulb designer or the electrician, you may only play a specific role.

In larger organizations, few people, if any, understand all the parts of the organization. If we model a large organization with many black boxes, then we can better understand it because we don't have to worry about all the details. Encapsulation is a handy modeling concept to hide complexity.

Abstraction

Sometimes we may not even want to model the black box within the system. For example, if your organization works with vendors, you may not want to model each one, even if they could be encapsulated in black boxes. A vendor may not fall within your system scope. More importantly, you could switch to a different vendor in the future.

Remember when we talked about how to model services earlier? We can use that same concept to abstract a vendor as an independent service, not having to worry about what happens inside that service. If we model it as an abstraction, although the underlying implementation of the service could change, the change won't affect our model.

A word about how encapsulation and abstraction are closely related, but different: encapsulation refers to hiding the details. For example, you don't really care how a car works as long as you can drive it. Abstraction refers to generalizing. For example, whether you drive a car, a truck or a motorcycle, there are some concepts such as braking, turning, accelerating, and ignition, that are common to them all.

Modularity

Many times, there are parts of the system that can be reused in different places. For example, a home appliance organization that sells many different products may be structured along product lines such as dishwashers, refrigerators, washing machines, and microwaves. However, the power supplies used across these products may be designed and produced by the same area within the organization. Therefore, as long as the interface for the power supply is properly specified, then the power supply becomes a modular component that different appliances can be plugged in to. In addition to such reusability, the concept of modularity also makes it easy to configure a larger system by combining smaller modules in different ways, much like how a LEGO toy model is constructed.

Large-scale software systems are typically built by assembling together many smaller modules, which in turn are made up of more modules, and so on. The following model illustrates this concept where the same module is used in multiple places.

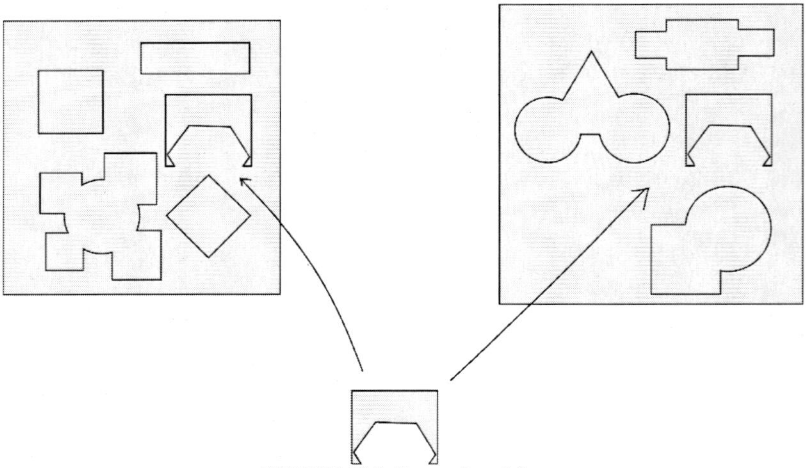

FIGURE 10-1: Reuse of modules

The concept of modularity is not restricted to physical parts. It can be used on intangible parts as well, such as software.

For example, encryption is a common module that is used in many places. If you'd like to encrypt data, you can use the same encryption module each time. If you want to upgrade the encryption module or fix a problem (bug) in it, you can simply make the change in one place and all the other modules that consume this one will automatically receive the new functionality.

The following example shows how Amazon can switch out its

shipping providers if desired, because the interface to the shipping service provider still remains the same.

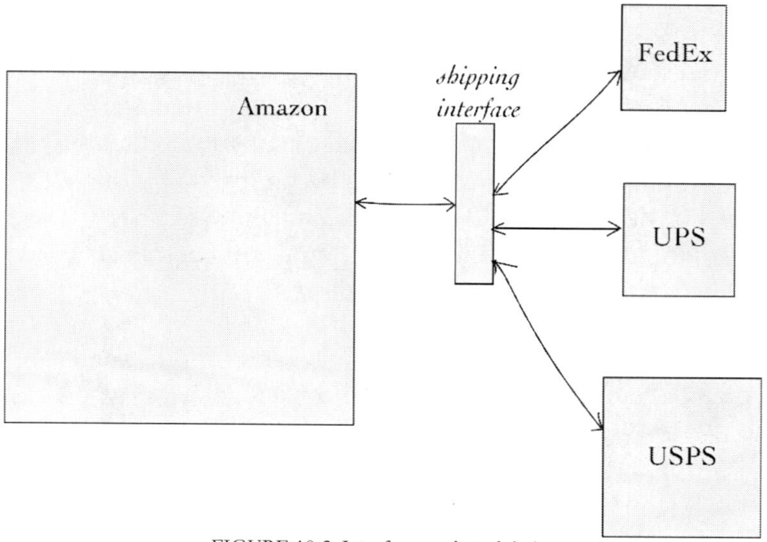

FIGURE 10-2: Interfaces and modularity

On the other hand, if your organization has a strong dependency on a vendor, then you will want to make note of it. Perhaps in the future you'd like to lessen the dependency. In that case, the current and future states can be modeled to illustrate this desire. The example below clearly shows the stronger coupling in the current state compared to the looser coupling in the future. Such a model helps to convey what the desired business of the future should look like.

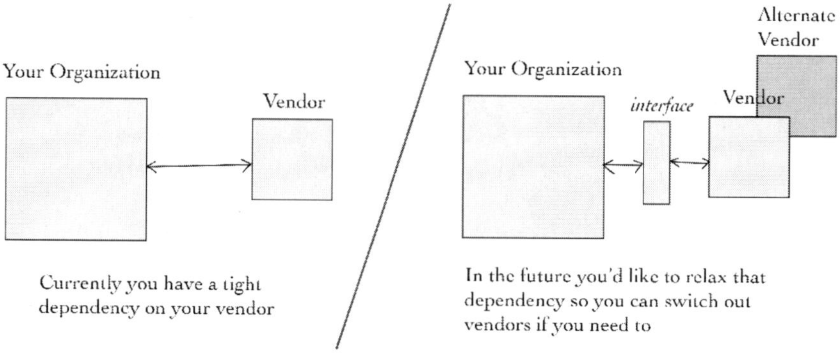

FIGURE 10-3: Loose coupling illustration

Inheritance

You may come across some fundamental processes in your organization that were developed to deal with specific situations.

Take hiring new employees, for example. All new employees may be subject to a basic background check. However, managers may be subject to some additional background checks since they have to manage employees. A new executive being hired may have to go through a basic background check, a manager background check, and an additional check required specifically for executives, since they may be privy to confidential information.

A person who works for IT, on the other hand, might need to go through a different kind of security clearance check beyond the basic check.

This is the concept of inheritance, where the background check of the executive "inherits" something from the manager background check and encompasses additional work on top of that.

The following model represents these processes:

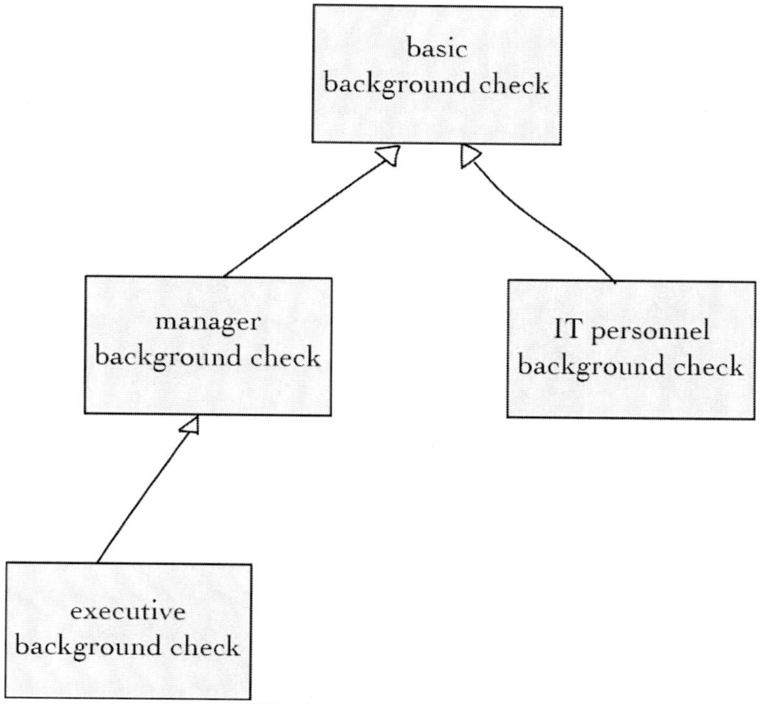

FIGURE 10-4: Concept of inheritance

Notice that the arrowheads are depicted with outlines rather than solid fills. This is the standard way to represent inheritance relationships, but do not worry about that now. Focus on what you are trying to understand.

Here's another example. Consider water. It's a specific type of liquid but inherits many of the general properties of liquids. All liquids exhibit viscosity and surface tension, take the shape of the container, etc. Yet the specific properties of water such as boiling point, density, etc., are different from many other liquids.

On the left in the diagram below, water is shown as a specific type of liquid. On the right is a different representation from which you can infer that water is a specific type of liquid. To explain the concept in the picture on the left, you don't have to necessarily worry about other liquids, while to show the same concept using the method on the right, you have to include examples of other liquids.

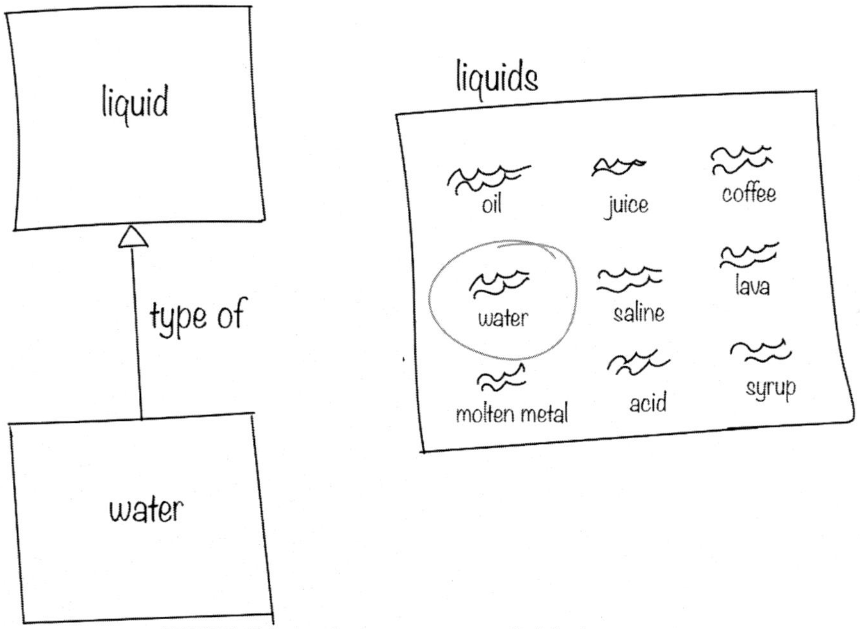

FIGURE 10-5: Another way to represent the inheritance concept

Association

An association is a powerful concept that can be used to indicate the relationship between two entities. These entities are connected in some meaningful way that you need to understand. So, you can just draw a line from one entity to another and label that line. If the relationship is obvious to you, you don't have to necessarily label the line, but labeling helps.

In an association, the two elements are independent yet related. For example, a computer is associated with a display. They can, of course, exist independently, but they are related as shown below. These are just two variations of drawing relationships, and you can use either one. The second, by depicting the objects with more detail, makes the model more interesting and obvious. Most times, I prefer the second way.

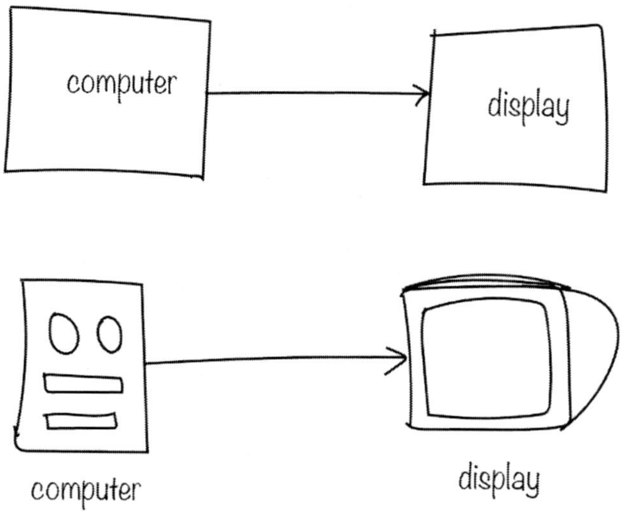

FIGURE 10-6: An association representation

The following are some variations you can find in association models:

Dependency: One element depends on the other in the sense that a change in one element affects the other. The maximum speed at which you drive on the highway depends on the speed limit posted.

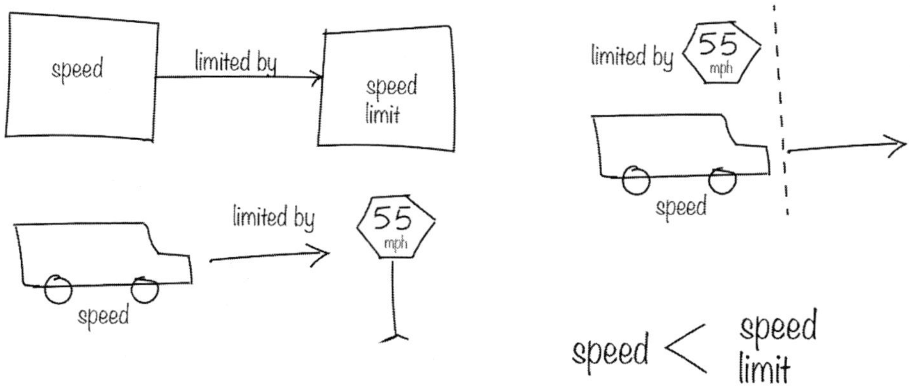

FIGURE 10-7: Dependency relationships

These visuals illustrate different ways to represent the speed of a vehicle that is restricted by the speed limit. There are even more possibilities than this, which you can depict creatively. The essence of the concept is to communicate the dependency relationship.

Contains: One element is contained within or makes up parts of another element. A book, for example, contains pages, and the book is what groups the pages together.

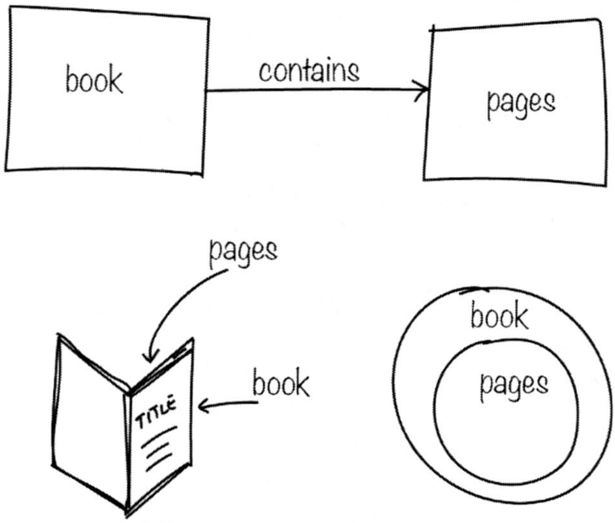

FIGURE 10-8: Container relationship concept

Realization: One element provides a specification that another model element implements. A business might need a mechanism to manage information about its customers, but the realization of that function could be through a notebook, a database, or something else.

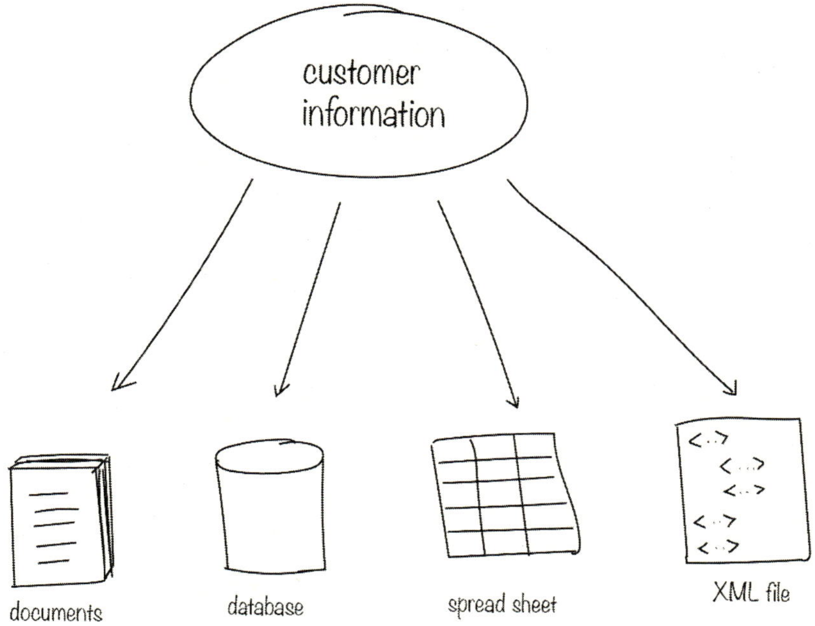

FIGURE 10-9: Realization concept

Transformation: Sometimes we want to show the transformation of one element to another or a change in state. An employee of your organization may have to pass an exam to get certified, for example. Before the exam, the employee is not certified. After the exam, they are.

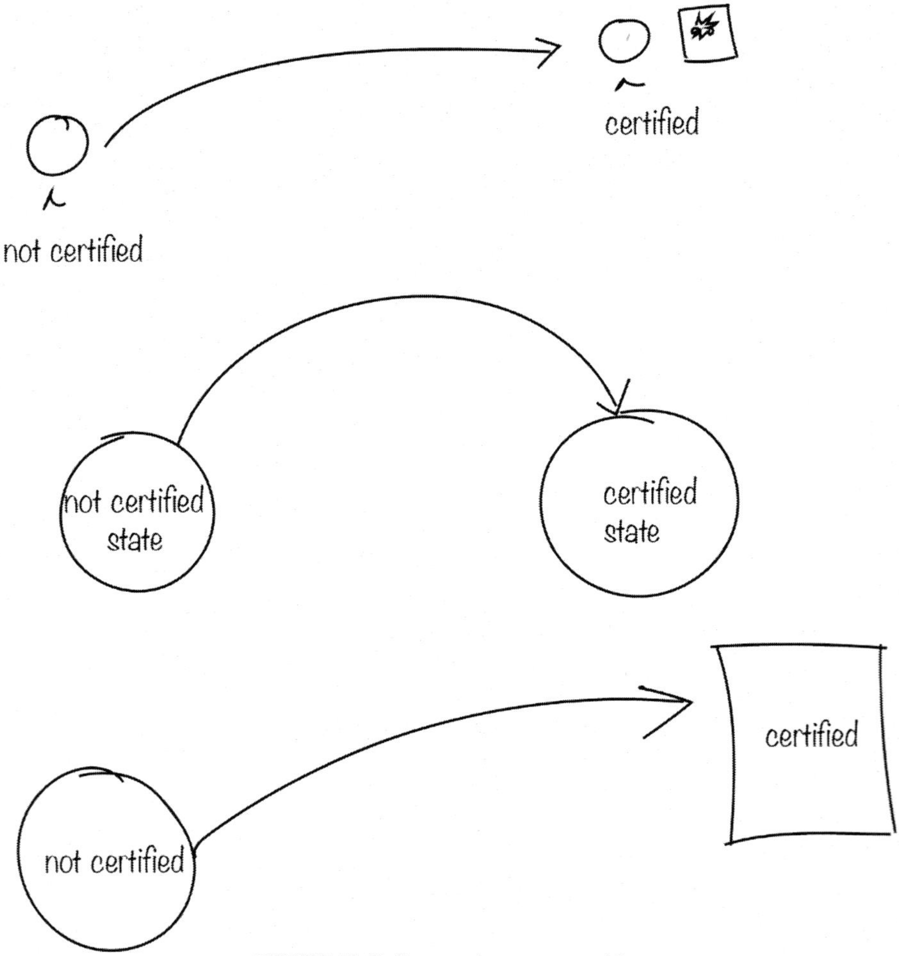

FIGURE 10-10: Representing a state transition

Composite Elements

Once you understand the basic elements of modeling, you can combine them to represent more complex concepts. For example, if you want to show siloed functional areas within your organization, you can draw rectangles as such:

FIGURE 10-11: Representing functional silos

Then let's say that you want to show how a customer's request cuts through the many siloed areas, which you can do like this:

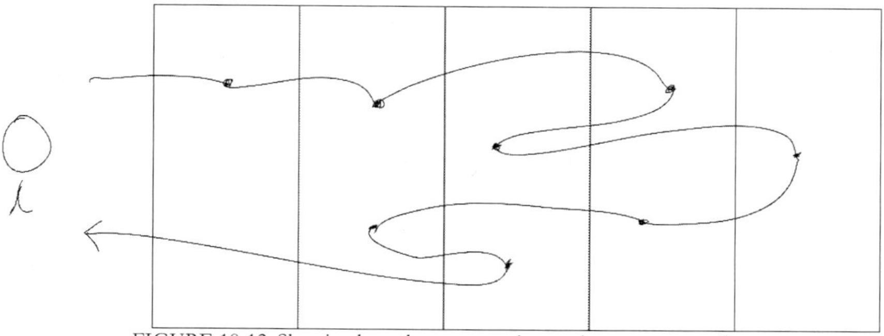

FIGURE 10-12: Showing how the customer interaction cuts across silos

Basic elements illustrate a complex concept. Now you can bring attention to the fact that these siloed areas have to work with one another to service the customer's request. You might also capture how long it takes for the customer's request to be fulfilled and distribute that time across the siloed areas appropriately. Then we'll know where the time is being spent. Some tasks obviously take more time, and not everything can be done quickly, but this gives managers a mechanism to help them look at the full picture and make some decisions. They'll know that it may not make sense to save a few minutes in one area, while another part of the process takes a few days. This model provides an overall perspective for decision making.

Events and Transitions

Some domains are best modeled with events, transitions, and states. Such a model is called a *state transition diagram*.

Take the simple case of a person who is applying for a bank loan. First, they do research. Then they pick the loan type they want, submit an application, get approved, and finally get the loan. Here's a state diagram that shows this process.

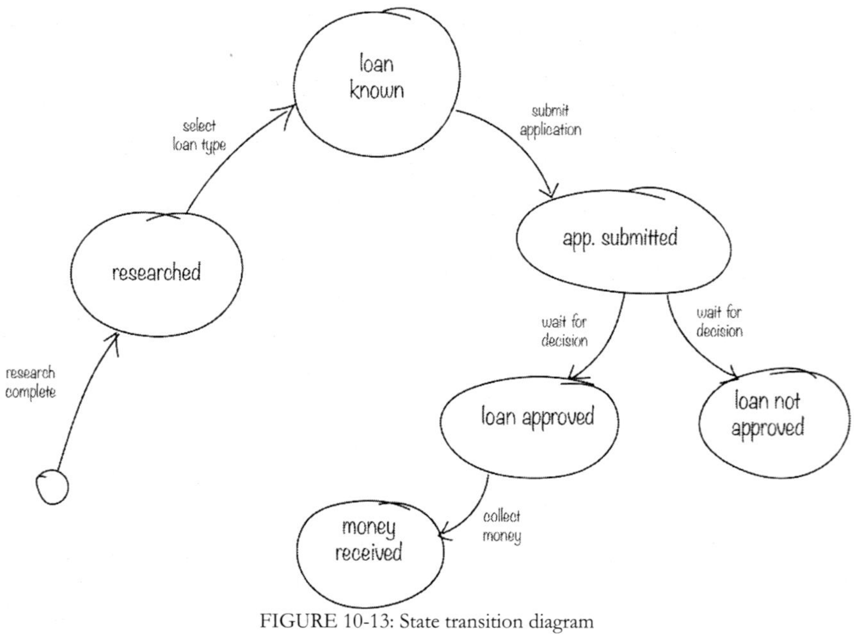

FIGURE 10-13: State transition diagram

Different people can be in different states at the same time. Tom may be in the "researched" state, while Lisa is in the "app. submitted" state. The state is usually captured by a noun, while the transition is captured by a verb. Thus, a person moves from a "loan known" state to an "app. submitted" state after taking the action of submitting the application form.

A state diagram is a great model to use when your focus is on a particular object that goes through different states. For example, if you want to model a person transitioning through different stages in life—baby, child, teen, young adult, mature adult, and senior—you can use a state transition diagram as a representation.

Sankey Diagrams

These diagrams are used to show how something can drop off at different points in time or at different places.

In budgeting, for example, your company will have a fixed amount of money that is distributed to functional areas. If there is a priority among these areas, then you can envision that distribution to look something like the following. Here the company starts out with a certain amount of money, and as the money is distributed, its loses more and more of it.

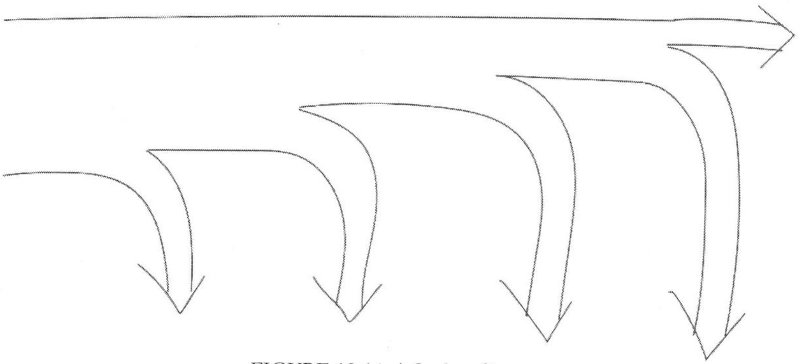

FIGURE 10-14: A Sankey diagram

Catch All—Creative Models

So far, I have introduced different ways to model your ecosystem. I have not covered every possible situation, but this is where you can apply your creativity. Remember that the intent of modeling your ecosystem is for you to understand it clearly. As you browse through and experiment with these modeling techniques, you will begin to recognize patterns and different ways to model. So, you can start to create your own tools to model any situation.

When nothing else works, you may even use text. However, be careful not to use too much text, because if you do, then it might become a document, and that's what we are trying not to make.

11. Bringing It All Together

We have learned a lot about modeling concepts. As you think through how to model your ecosystem, here are some guidelines you may find useful.

How Detailed Should Your Model Be?

As you model your ecosystem, you will capture some details but not all. How much detail you capture depends on what you want to understand about your ecosystem. As an initial step, you can just capture the elements in your ecosystem at a high level. Then you can drill down into details.

This video gives you an idea of what that can look like.

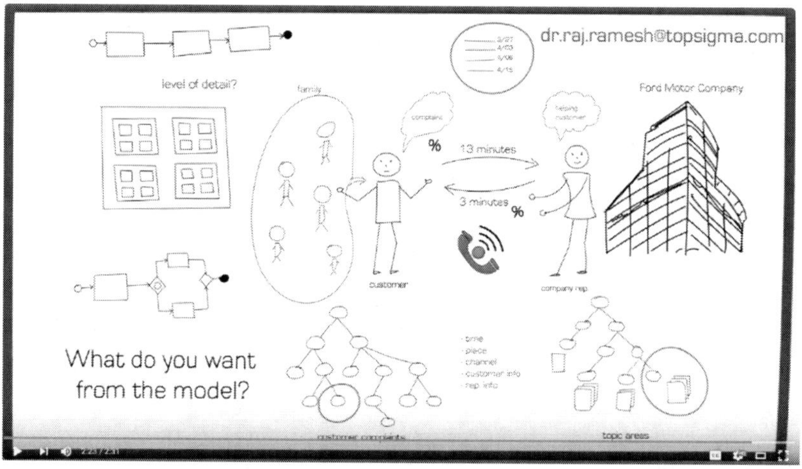

FIGURE 11-1: Video: modeling the ecosystem

Since you play multiple roles in your life—an employee, a parent, a coach, etc.—you might create a different model for each of these roles. Even at work if you play several roles—such as mentor, manager, employee, etc.—you may end up creating a separate model for each role and capturing the ecosystem around that role.

One way to start modeling is to identify your skills. Why does your company need you? The answer to this question leads you to how you fit within your organization. By modeling your skills and the value that you can bring to the company relative to what the company needs, you are in a better position to communicate those critical aspects to your manager.

Steps to Creating a Model

So far, we have discussed the importance of modeling and the principles around it. I will briefly discuss the actual steps you can take to come up with a good model. I purposely use bullet points instead of numbers below to emphasize that these steps are just quasi-sequential, which means that you can go back and forth among them.

- Identify the elements of interest. These will be defined by the question you are trying to answer. At this stage you will also define your scope, the ecosystem. What do you want to know or understand from it?

- Identify characteristics of the elements—size, type, owner, function, etc.
- Sort and group similar information.
- Try to identify how certain elements "fit" with other elements. A good way to do this is to look at two elements at a time and think about how they could be connected directly, if at all. Don't worry if you don't get all of this right away; you can always refine the model as you learn more.
- Draw a picture with your elements and their relationships to each other. Initially the elements can be represented as simple circles with text to name them. You may have a bunch of circles tagged with names. Then you can change the shape of these circles to reflect the elements that you are trying to capture, like replacing a box that represents a computer with a simple drawing of a computer.
- Whenever you have a thought you need to capture but don't know where it goes, or you just want to capture it without assigning it a place, jot it down as a note on the diagram.
- Look at the picture and see if you have to rearrange anything. If so, just scope out what should go where.
- Now start circling concepts you want to convey, and the story behind the picture.
- Refine and iterate.

The power of your visual depiction is that you've managed to pack a lot of information on a single page, and you've also illustrated how different elements are connected.

An Example: Driverless Cars

As I discussed in Part I, we are living in a fast-changing world. The advent of driverless cars is one of those changes. I'll list some prompts to help you figure out the answer to the question, "How will driverless cars affect me?"

Let's figure out the thought process you'd use to identify the things you need to consider in your ecosystem. Here's the scenario:

Driverless cars will be on the roads soon. These are cars built on AI technologies. The rate at which driverless cars will be introduced on the roads will be gradual. First a few people will use them, and then more and then even more. It will probably take close to ten years before 90 percent of the cars in the U.S. are driverless. Let's think about aspects of this scenario so we can model it to get a sense of what the future will be like. Here are some of the questions we need to think about deeply:

- What will the rate of introduction be?
- What changes do we need to make to the road infrastructure?
- How will fueling stations need to change?
- Will cab driving as a profession disappear?
- If you are an Uber driver, will you begin to lose revenue?
- What about trucks that move a majority of the goods across the country? How will the trucking industry change?
- What goes inside a self-driving car? Software, electronics, entertainment, connectivity, etc.?
- How will riders spend their time, now that they don't have to worry about driving?
- Will the traffic become better or worse?
- How will cars with drivers and driverless cars coexist on the same roads? Will there be separate lanes?
- Will this technology be applied in other areas as well—like

agricultural equipment, earthmovers, or even residential lawn mowers?

- Will people even need to get driver's licenses? How will that system change?
- How will parking lots and structures need to change? Will the number of parking lots be reduced?
- Will people own cars or rent them whenever they need to? Who will own the cars?
- How will these cars be insured? Who pays for the insurance—the owning companies or the passengers?
- Will insurance cover software glitches?
- Will accidents decline, leading to fewer traffic deaths and injuries?
- What will happen when cars are hacked?
- How will the jobs of people associated with cars change? These include traffic police, lawyers, car salespeople, mechanics, etc.
- When travel becomes easier, will there be more vehicles or fewer vehicles on the road? What about the effects of pollution?
- What new government rules and regulations can be anticipated?
- What forms of competition can disrupt the use of driverless cars?
- Will driverless cars be practical in other countries where roads may be narrower or have no clearly marked lanes, or where people and animals frequently walk across the middle of the road?

These questions can help us think through the ecosystem we'd like to model. You can also group the questions into categories to think through them systematically.

How to Model Anything

Can you model almost anything? How about intangible things like leadership? The answer is yes. If you can think it, you can model it.

What about abstract things like creativity of leaders? When we look at different leaders, if we have a sense of who is more creative, then it is possible to model this trait. For example, we could draw stick figures of these people and draw a circle around their heads to indicate their levels of creativity. The larger the circle, the more creative they are.

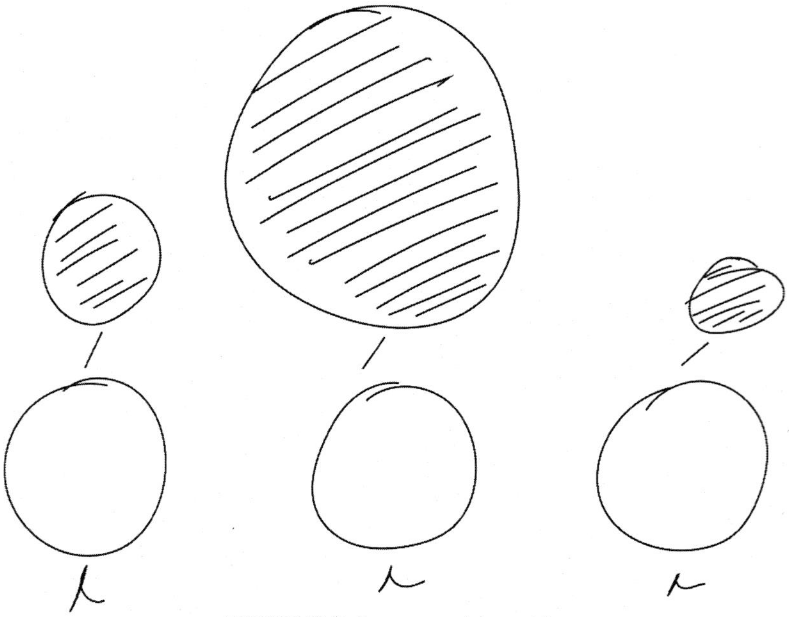

FIGURE 11-2: A way to model creativity

I already discussed this in an earlier section about modeling the abstract. The point is, you can model almost anything, and if no visual or tool comes to mind, just use words as a substitute until you develop your skills. You will get better with time.

Why I Use Videos

To help you with the tools and techniques I've shared here, you can refer to more of my videos. I start with a blank page and slowly build up the model as I narrate the story behind the visual. This should help you understand how to essentially create your models from a blank sheet.

Since this is a much more effective way of communicating these tactics, I encourage you to check out my YouTube channel, **www.youtube.com/rajramesh**, and watch a few videos.

PART III: TAKE ACTION—HOW CAN YOU ADAPT?

In Part I, we talked about awareness and specifically how the ecosystem around you is changing. In Part II, we talked about ways to model the ecosystem. In Part III, we will learn how to take action so you can improve your ecosystem and be prepared for change.

12. The Process

The process of adapting to a new ecosystem is a set of simple steps:

(1) Gather information.

(2) Model the ecosystem.

(3) Analyze and act on the information.

This part will be organized along these lines, and I will provide examples as we go along. Some examples use full-scale contexts, which I will call macro-ecosystems, and others use narrow contexts, which I will call micro-ecosystems. Think of a micro-ecosystem as zooming in to one particular aspect of the macro-ecosystem to see the details. Using the macro- and micro-ecosystems, you will be able to see the big picture as well as the details, and easily switch context between the two extremes to home in on your areas of interest.

To make this more concrete with an example, consider how Steve Jobs ran Apple. Apple is a huge company in which there are a lot of things to do. Jobs obviously would not have had the time or energy to focus on all aspects, from hiring good people, to engineering design, to manufacturing, to customer experience, and so on. Rather, he was able to take a global view of the company and delegate the things that he was not interested in or did not have expertise in to other people. At the same time, he could focus on the product design and customer experience, something that he had a deep interest in. Design and customer experience happened to be some of the most critical parts of Apple that made the company so successful and helped establish a cultlike following among its customers.

Likewise, it is important to think through and analyze the components of your own ecosystem at different scales.

From Data to Knowledge at Your Organization

Today we have easy access to tons of data. Let's say I want to understand business strategy. I do a Google search on this term, and it turns up over forty-one million results (as of December 21, 2018). That's way too much data for me to sort through to figure out what is important and what is not. I end up reading the first couple of articles. If I want to really understand the concept of business strategy, though, I may have to seek an expert or read a book on the topic. Often, while we have a lot of data and information at our fingertips, what we lack is clarity of thought and understanding.

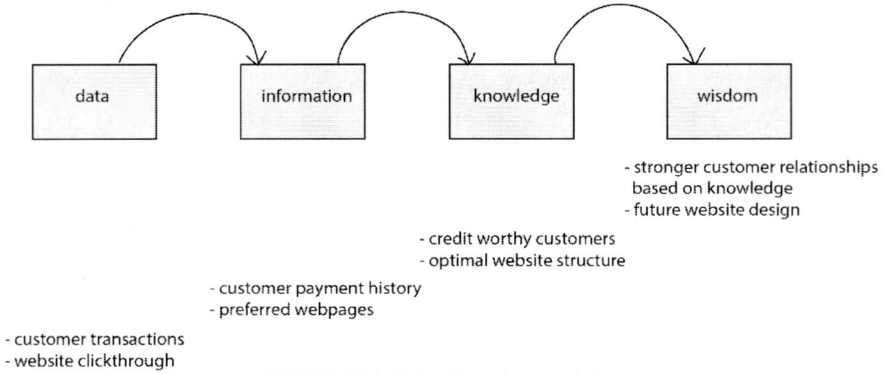

FIGURE 12-1: Going from data to wisdom

The picture above shows an evolution along the spectrum from data to wisdom. Today, many companies collect data in abundance. But it has been difficult to leverage that data for knowledge. The construction of knowledge from data requires organizing such data as models.

Picking up on the concept of business strategy again, you have to do more than read a few articles about it to truly understand and internalize it; you have to build a model. If the concepts are simple, you already build models intuitively in your head (often called mental models). If the concepts are more complex, you need to create visual models of the concepts.

Initially the mental model you build may be weak, but as you read more, talk to experts, and gain experience with developing and using business strategy, your mental model keeps getting better and more robust. The stronger it gets, the more able you are to leverage your knowledge effectively. This is the essence of learning. In learning, you refine and build your mental model until you understand it thoroughly and internalize it.

When a concept is presented to several people, each of them creates their own mental model of the same concept. That's why it is possible for two people to provide two different answers to the same question. But having different mental models for the same concept is often problematic. In an organization where decisions are made by consensus, arriving at a decision will be difficult if different people have different mental models. There are two primary reasons for ending up with differing mental models of the same information. (1) When information is used to create models, the consumer (or builder) might selectively choose information to build the model. (2) Different consumers are exposed to a different set of model possibilities, and hence they might end up creating differing models using the same information.

The following picture illustrates how five people think about the same concept in five different ways—some visually, some as text, and some as sounds:

FIGURE 12-2: Different people might have different mental models

How then can we hope to get everybody's thinking aligned?

The examples will cover a broad range of business topics.

Sometimes I will focus on AI and sometimes I will discuss general business concepts. Through these examples, we will understand how to create models that capture the essence of what you would like to understand.

13. Gathering Information

If you want to understand and model your ecosystem, you have to gather information. Here are some ways to do that and to document it. This is similar to how you would, say, research which camera to buy. It's important to write things down as you find new material, because most of us easily forget details. I definitely do. We also don't want to write a novel, but capture the gist of our thoughts. One of the most effective methods I've used is "visual note taking," which I will discuss soon.

Let's look at some ways to gather information.

Information can be gathered through reading, observing, or listening. While some is gathered through experience, I will focus on these methods. Each person who uses these information-gathering processes will inevitably read, observe, and listen in different ways. The models each person builds will be distinctly shaped by those differences.

In all modes of gathering information—reading, observing, and listening—strengthening your skills in visual note taking is beneficial. Unlike typing notes, taking visual notes with a pen and paper or a drawing program on a tablet gives you two dimensions instead of one line of text, which in turn provides a much richer way to capture nuances. Visual note taking is also much more powerful than simple linear note taking because it allows you to consume information much more actively.

An example of some of the techniques I use to make this process easy is in an article I wrote called "How I Capture Notes Effectively and Electronically."[26]

---

[26] Raj Ramesh, "How I Capture Ideas Effectively and Electronically," *LinkedIn Pulse,* December 20, 2017, https://www.linkedin.com/pulse/how-i-capture-notes-effectively-electronically-raj-ramesh/.

While it is not the focus of this book, I do want to highlight some of the main techniques in order to make model building easier. As you gather information from multiple sources through reading, observing, and listening, you should learn how to capture this information in the most effective way possible.

There is a big difference between acquiring the information and capturing it effectively. When acquiring information, you may simply write down what you are learning without interpreting it, understanding it, or being critical. This is a mindless activity of documenting information, which doesn't engage your cognitive abilities. Unbeknownst to themselves, people who type out notes in a meeting often just capture the words being shared without processing the meaning or intent of the conversations.

In order for information to be captured more effectively, it must go through your cognitive brain, which will analyze and process it. The notes you take may not be verbatim, but you will understand the meaning of the information in them. This is most important. A single page of visual notes can often be more effective than ten pages of typed text.

There is abundant free information on visual note taking.[27]

Reading Effectively

Read actively for understanding, taking notes and drawing pictures. This is most effective for information retention. Try to relate new information to concepts you already know. This sort of "pegging" is how you build your knowledge of the subject and also comes in handy when you begin to develop the model of your ecosystem.

Maintain a running list of questions that you need to seek answers

---

[27] See Kathy Schrock, "Sketchnoting," *Kathy Schrock's Guide to Everything,* accessed October 11, 2016, http://www.schrockguide.net/sketchnoting.html and "Visual Notetaking," *Show What You Know with Media,* accessed December 22, 2016, http://showwithmedia.com/visual-notetaking/.

for. As you proceed to gather more information, you'll think of more questions that need to be answered. Add those to your running question list.

Consuming Written Information Efficiently

To consume a lot of information in the most efficient way, you need to have a general idea of the ecosystem you want to collect information on and are reading about. Skim a document first to see if it is relevant, and then read the details. If it has a table of contents, browse through that. Flip through the pages and read samples. Look at the chapter headings to get an idea of the structure of the content. Read the introduction to get an idea of what the document covers. Skim the rest of the document and try to understand the information it provides in the context of what you already know. Does it look too complex, too simple, or just right? If it's too complex, perhaps you can come back to it later. If it's too simple, it may not be worth your time.

There will be different types of documents for any ecosystem, and each will require different strategies to consume them. To get the gist of the document's content, read actively by taking notes or drawing pictures to understand concepts.

As you consume more documents, you'll want to build a plan to organize concepts. This is not a table of contents, but a two-dimensional visual of how concepts are related to each other.

In some cases, documents are readily accessible (such as an internal company document or a URL), while in others, you will have to keep a record of where you found them. Sometimes you can just take down the title, author, publication, and year to find it again. Sometimes you might want to make a copy—provided the material is not copyrighted. With today's cheap memory, rather than making a physical copy, you may want to simply take a picture or scan the document and organize it on your computer's hard drive. Just be cautious about making copies of documents with the intent to read them, but then never having the time to get to them. That's as bad as not having the document to reference in the first place.

As you read more, you might be able to identify the major categories the documents fall into. You can then organize this content into such categories. There is no hard-and-fast rule on this—just do what makes sense, much like how you organize emails. If you find that you are not adept at organizing documents, talk to a friend who may be better at it than you are. Organizing online material is no different, and you can use the same techniques. Just be sure that you don't get distracted by links within the page and go off tangentially into Useless Browsing Land. You can easily save links to articles in your browser by adding them to favorites and organizing them into folders.

Material Types

Most organizations have an abundance of documentation. To understand the ecosystem, you'll only have to access the organization's documents and read them. Types of documents may include project charters, trade journals, blogs, business books, memorandums, user guides, process guides, technical manuals, architectural documents, etc. However, you'll probably find that most of these documents were written in isolation and over time. Your task is to read them to build a "global table of contents" in your own mind as you consume the information.

Some of the problems you could encounter with these documents are that they are outdated, too detailed, or too shallow; some might be filled with platitudes; some may be abstract; and some may be written by multiple people with different styles of writing. As you read through documents and construct a model of how all the pieces are connected, you'll find some gaps in your model that you'll have to fill through some other means—such as talking with people—if you want your model to be reliable and complete for your purposes.

You should also look at articles and books written outside the walls of your organization. You might want to understand the external factors that influence the elements in your ecosystem. Magazines, newspaper articles, and trade and technical journals can be useful if you want to consider many perspectives.

These sources, however, often have fragmented coverage, focusing on areas of interest to their audiences. You'll have to learn to read critically and question everything, looking for evidence that supports the writer's point of view.

Observing with Intent

Chance favors only the prepared mind.

—Louis Pasteur, biologist

Keen observation is a critical skill for understanding your ecosystem. Observation is a main source of information because a large portion of what you'll want to understand about the ecosystem is not written down. Understanding culture or politics, for example, mostly comes through observation. Observation can also help to either substantiate an argument or disprove it. In many organizations, you'll find vision statements, organizational themes, and principles pasted on the wall. However, in some organizations, these are mere platitudes; through your observation you may conclude that the writing is in conflict with what actually goes on.

In one large organization, statements such as "Customer needs come first" and "Employees are our most important resource" were plastered on the walls, but if you were to observe the sentiments of people interacting with customers or the leadership stances, you could easily tell that these statements were empty words. The attitude was more about "We take advantage of the customer when we can" and "If employees are not aggressively selling, we need to fire them." This data about misalignment can come through observation.

Visual and Mental Processing

Observation is much more than simply seeing something; it an active cognitive process. All observations have two elements: (1)

perception, which is usually visual, and (2) mental processing, which is the partly conscious and partly unconscious absorption of that information.

Sometimes you might have to put two observations together to get a full picture. For example, when someone says, "I notice that my stomach gets upset when I eat spicy food," there are two observations involved that they have connected by using a mental process. By themselves, the observations may not be that useful. However, in combination, they provide more useful information. As the number of such discrete observations increases, the number of combinations through which they can be connected can grow exponentially. Hence expertise, prior experience, heuristics, and intuition may help to identify a small set of knowledge, which can then help you decide which actions to take. If you have identified the connection between spicy food and an upset stomach, you may want to avoid spicy food in the future.

In the model developed by French physiologist Claude Bernard, such connection making is necessary for creativity.[28] Bernard came up with two types of observations: (1) passive observations, which are unexpected, and (2) active observations, which are done deliberately. We perform the former a lot, and rightly so, because actively observing all the time would tire out our brain. However, in our passive observation, if we notice something of interest or out of place, or if we tie it to our existing knowledge, then the observation may turn active, in which case we focus our attention on it. This is when new knowledge or perspective is gained.

So, determining what to observe actively becomes important. This is what differentiates the keen observer from the casual one.

Cultivating Observational Skills

Studies have shown that observational skills can be cultivated by

---

[28] "Claude Bernard," *Wikipedia*, accessed September 11, 2016, https://en.wikipedia.org/w/index.php?title=Claude_Bernard&oldid=738841522.

watching things with an active and inquiring mind. In fact, directly observing something is more important than a large accumulation of information through other means. Observation helps you infer the prevailing sentiments of people—be they your coworkers, those who report to you directly, your friends, or your customers. You can develop the capacity for pattern recognition, which depends on a broad range of networked knowledge and allows you to spot things that are out of place.

If you have first read some documents to understand your ecosystem, you have some foundation to work from. Using observation to see patterns, you can confirm or negate the information you have read. Since you have prior knowledge of what to look for, observation may become easier for those domains. For example, if you read that new employees in your organization go through an onboarding process, but when you talk to such employees you find that they don't complete it or complain about the inadequacy of information given at onboarding, you may conclude that either the onboarding process does not exist or it is ineffective. You can then further delve into that problem to understand what's going on.

Just as you can train yourself in other activities, you can train yourself to become a better observer. At first this may be conscious and laborious, much like learning how to ride a bicycle, but as time goes on, it will become habitual and natural. Effective observation also requires you to build up your knowledge of the subject, because if you don't have the knowledge, then your observations will not yield much. Towards this end, you should start learning more about how your organization works. This knowledge builds on itself. The more you understand, the better your observations; and the better your observations, the more you'll understand about your organization.

Techniques for Improving Observational Skills

A friend, Bob, recently went on a diet. His restriction was that he could have only 500 calories a day for the first two weeks. Prior to the diet, Bob had scarfed food down. Suddenly, the healthy foods he ate during his diet—which were mostly fruits and vegetables—tasted a lot more delicious. Since food was "scarce," he started to relish each bite and really taste the flavors. He said that he identified flavors that he "never thought existed!" Since he was forced to focus on what he ate, and since it was limited in quantity, he became conscious of the taste. The same is true of observation. If you take your time to "smell the roses," you will increase your observation skills.

Be engaged in what you are observing. Try to notice the finer details. If you are observing people, look (sometimes discretely) at their facial expressions, and try to figure out what is not being said. Notice any fidgety movements or sideways glances (perhaps at their bosses).

Practice by picking something to observe every day. Perhaps you often have lunch by yourself in the cafeteria. That's a great place to observe people. See who is talking to whom. What are their facial expressions? Who is complaining? Who is speaking well of their work?

If observing is difficult, try to take notes of your observations. You can even draw or doodle what's going on. Try to recall what you observed at a later point in time. Did you notice anything unusual? Can you remember if the person you were observing had glasses on? Did you hear and can you remember what they were talking about? What was the color of the person's outfit?

Practice connecting the dots. Can you relate what you heard in the morning to something you heard later during the day? In a status meeting, can you listen to what people are working on and try to put the whole picture together? How is what Adam is working on related to what Betty is working on, and how are both related to what David is working on? Does it make sense? If not, can you ask someone else to help you understand better? Do you find any gaps in the work as a whole?

Constantly strive to increase your knowledge of the ecosystem. The best observations come when you have some foundational knowledge to leverage. That is why observation and knowledge feed off each other. The more knowledge you have, the more effective your observations will be.

Be engaged. Be part of the scene.

Listening Actively

Listening is one of the most difficult things to do—especially for extroverts. Often, we don't listen as well as we should because we're distracted by other things in the environment, such as the television, the internet, our mobile phones, thinking about what we're going to have for dinner, or something else. Even worse, we think we're listening to the other person, but we're really not giving them our full attention.

Many experts say that the more you speak, the less you will learn. Listening is, of course, another important skill for gathering information. The person you are speaking with may have information that is not covered in any document, information that may be critical for your complete understanding of the ecosystem.

Active listening is the act of not only hearing what is being said but also attempting to comprehend the meaning of it. In this mode of listening, the listener often gives visual feedback to the speaker as an indication that they understand what is being shared. The listener may also paraphrase the content as a further confirmation of understanding.

Techniques for Listening

Here are some of the techniques to help you become an active listener.

As you are listening, try to absorb the content and frame the information in your own mind. This way, you can try to restate what the speaker said and get confirmation that you understood the information. You can also try to summarize the conversation.

We can listen faster than the speaker can speak, and this causes our brains to have some free time. During this time, our thoughts may wander, or we may access other information that is irrelevant to the topic. Perhaps something the speaker said triggered a thought in our mind. We then want to introduce this thought into the conversation, which interrupts the flow from the speaker. If you have a thought, write it down or try to remember it so you can bring it up later. Do not let these thoughts interrupt the speaker.

You can also actively show that you are listening by nodding your head or prompting the speaker with words like "Um-hmm" or "Yes?"

After the speaker has finished a line of thought, share your initial thoughts on the information, such as observations, insights, and experiences. Then listen carefully to confirm that your insights are on target.

If you have young kids, try practicing by listening intently to what they have to say. This will serve a dual purpose of helping you practice and also building a good relationship with your children!

Try to read the emotion of the speaker. Are they feeling happiness, satisfaction, anger, pride, frustration, etc.?

While it is important for you to understand "where the speaker has been," it is often just as important to understand where they see themselves in the future. This helps you get a sense of how the ecosystem is poised to change. If you get the same reading from many people you talk to, you can get a general sense of changes, positive or negative.

Open-ended questions, of course, are always good because they do not constrain the speaker. In a few cases, the speaker may have difficulty starting, in which case it is best to have a general outline of the topics you'd like to cover, along with a breakdown of those topics. That way you can prompt the speaker without putting too much of a constraint on the direction of the conversation.

Pausing and silence are powerful tools, but they take a lot of practice. When there is dead air, some interviewers like to fill it with talking. On the other hand, if you let the speaker fill it first, you have given them the time to think through what needs to be shared. Perhaps the speaker needs time to organize their thoughts. Perhaps they're trying to recall what stories to share. If you feel really uncomfortable with silence, take a three-minute break using some excuse as a pretext. Leave the speaker alone. When you return, you'll often find them ready to share something new.

Don't talk about yourself. Let the speaker share, even if you have had more experiences than they have. Perhaps you will appreciate a different point of view. Give the speaker the stage, so to speak.

Some speakers can show signs of doubt or be aggressive, agitated, or angry. They may not even want you there in the first place. If negative feelings are directed towards you, then either ease out, saying that you'll meet with the person later, or change the direction of the conversation. If the emotions are directed towards the subject at hand, for instance about their experiences or their organization, you must tune in even more, because you'll want to understand their perspective.

Summary

As you can see, there are many ways to gather information. Most likely you'll be using more than one of them for any particular situation. These techniques give you guidance but are not prescriptive. Choose those techniques that will quickly provide the most relevant information you need.

14. Understanding your Ecosystem

Once you've gathered information, it's time to organize it through modeling. Modeling is the crux of understanding, so I will focus on it in greater detail. If your model is good, you can go back for more information to fill in any gaps, and then you can analyze the model more effectively.

Organizing the information that you gathered in the form of a document is typically not useful for our purposes. That's because a document is sequential, due to the nature of the medium. We want a more multidimensional understanding of the ecosystem, which is what we seek to achieve through modeling.

A prerequisite to understanding and modeling the ecosystem is understanding the principles of modeling.

If you are an artist and you want to paint a picture, you'll need a canvas, some brushes, and paint; you'll also need to understand some basic concepts of color, background, representation, perspective, etc. Likewise, to model the ecosystem you'll need to know some basic principles, techniques, and tools. These are the techniques I introduced in Part II of this book.

Examples of Your Ecosystems

When you go to the office, you work in a certain ecosystem. At your company, you interact with various elements in that ecosystem including people, processes, culture, computer systems, etc. Your company also interacts with other entities such as vendors, customers, business partners, etc.

Let's use another example. You drive your car to work every day—and each way takes up to an hour. You want to make your commute better. In your system, you'll include the car, the drive, what you do in the car while driving, the traffic, the parking, and anything else that is relevant to solving the problem. You can improve this system by perhaps taking the train instead of driving. That will save you money and give you more time to catch up on other things. You will lose some flexibility, but the overall system, measured by your priorities, may be better than the current one. In this case, your intent is to design a better system.

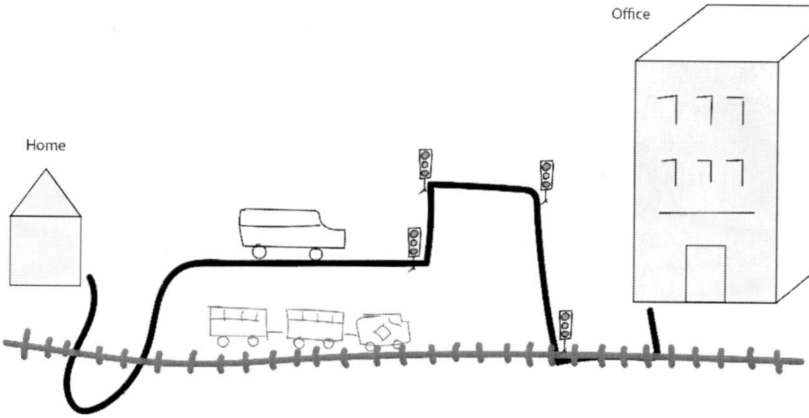

FIGURE 14-1: Doodle of your drive to work

Going back to your workplace, here are some of the elements you may find in your company:

- *Stakeholders:* customers, community, partners, competitors, vendors, investors, owners, regulators, staff, agents, etc.

- *Nontangible assets:* vision, strategy, business processes, business capabilities, decisions, metrics and measures, risk, governance, leadership, culture, business performance, branding, relationships, inflow and outflow of money, training, finances, information, intellectual property, services, models, reports, contracts, incentives, accounts, policies, rules, regulations, standards, bills and receipts, channels, ledgers, taxes, capacity, records, litigation/cases, solutions, tools, data, software applications, analysis, etc.

- *Tangible assets:* products, goods, facilities, real estate, furniture, means of transportation, supplies, computing hardware, etc.

When modeling your ecosystem, you may use one or more of the above elements. Is there a standard way to include these elements in your model? No. As we move forward, we will explore the different ways your model will use these elements.

Knowing Your Context

When you think about an ecosystem, context is also important. Let's frame context in terms of the concept called social identity. Consider a supermarket shopper, Adam. He could be a cook, the head of the family, an engineer, a coach for his son's baseball league, a customer for an insurance company, and a board member of his daughter's school—all at the same time. In other words, Adam can play multiple roles, and not every role is relevant all the time.

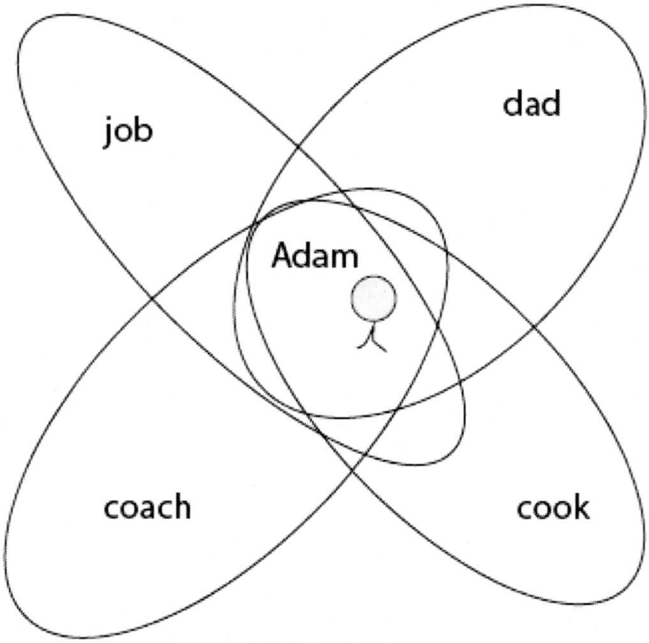

FIGURE 14-2: Framing the context

If the ecosystem you are interested in analyzing happens to be the baseball league, then Adam's role as his son's baseball coach is critical, but his other roles may be irrelevant, unless being a school board member has an influence on, say, the upkeep of the baseball field.

When you model the ecosystem, you have to consider the relevance of the different elements you include for analysis. Unfortunately, there is no way to truly know if you have included all the relevant elements. Analyzing and understanding the ecosystem is a continual exercise.

Most times, the ecosystem you are analyzing is dynamic and will continue to change. Your analysis, therefore, is a little more difficult.

An Office Example of Modeling

Now let's take a quick example from the workplace. I won't get into too much detail, since the idea here is to give you a flavor of how you can apply these principles.

You have just been given a new responsibility by your boss to drive a new project. The finance people have told your CEO that your profit margins have been decreasing in the last five years, and the leaders believe that this is due to higher operating costs. Your task is to identify where the money is going.

To do this properly, there are multiple factors to consider: who will be on your team, what skills they need, deliverables, timeline, whether you will take a phased approach, who needs to know the outcome, whether to share results incrementally, what actions the team needs to take, whether you can leverage existing data and documents, and so on.

If you draft a standard project plan with timelines and activities, a leadership audience might have a difficult time getting the full picture. The project plan is a tool and has its place, but not for quick informal communication. A project plan is also linear, which limits its scope.

Instead, you could communicate using a picture illustrating all of the relevant factors. This picture has context that readers can read as they would a map.

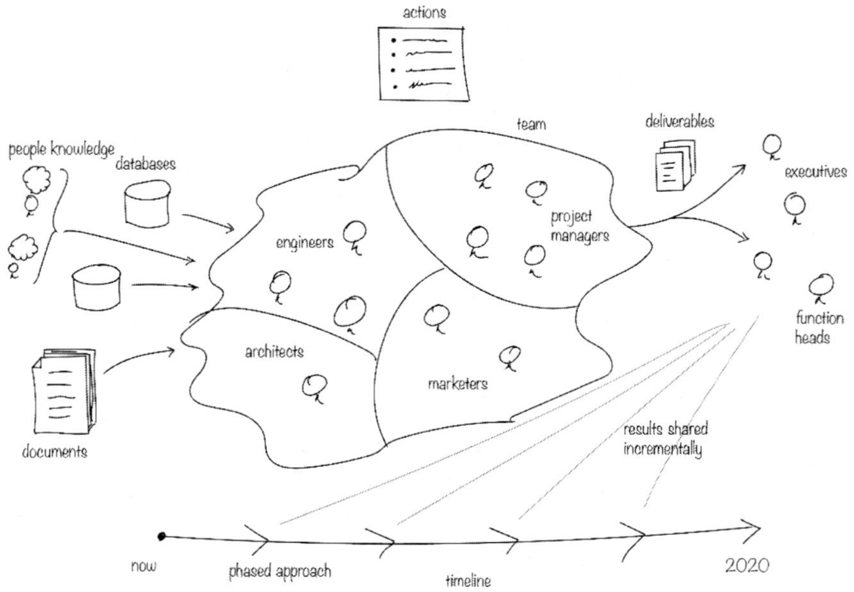

FIGURE 14-8: Modeling project management at an office

The visual above captures a lot of information on a single page. This is the type of visual that can help you understand and adapt to the ecosystem.

Seeing the Big Picture

Why do you need to see the big picture and how will do you it? Today's world is highly interconnected. The work you do may have huge implications across the globe. For example, the engineers who developed Twitter had no idea that it would enable the Arab Spring, changing the political and economic climate of an entire region.

At your workplace, what you do and what the organization does are tightly integrated. As your organization transforms, your role will change. How will you be affected by that change? Do you see yourself playing an important role in the transformed organization? How do you know if that will happen? Do you have the skills necessary for that new role?

To answer these questions, you need to understand your own role in that new future so you can quickly adapt and be relevant in your organization or outside of it.

Research has shown that an employee is much happier if they know their role in the organization and how they contribute to its success. With higher impact comes higher recognition, responsibilities, and fulfillment.

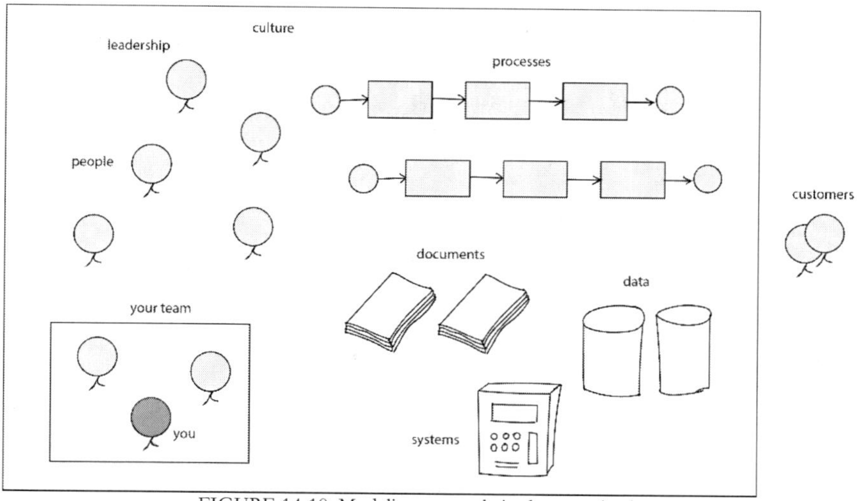

FIGURE 14-10: Modeling your role in the organization

You don't exist in isolation within your organization. You play a role in helping it fulfill its mission. In that capacity, you interact with other elements—such as people, machines, processes, etc.

By helping you to understand those interactions, your model will help you locate your place in the organization in relation to all these elements. The more you understand your role and your contribution, the easier it is to expand the scope of your role and have a bigger impact.

15. Example Systems and Their Visual Models

So far, we have covered the various ways to model the ecosystem around you, but now let's take a step back and look at some broader applications. Modeling has been around for a long time, though perhaps not in the terms we have used. In this section, we'll explore some examples of ecosystems and ways to model them, starting out with how the cave dweller modeled their ecosystem.

Cave Dweller Models

Imagine that you are a caveman (not to be chauvinistic, but most hunting was done by males at the time) planning to hunt down a woolly mammoth for dinner. Even though your language has not matured and you can only communicate in grunts and sounds, you need to corral your cavemates to buy in to your strategic plan. You draw pictures on the cave depicting how this attack should proceed—assigning a role to each person. You haven't seen the woolly mammoth yet, but you need to communicate about what to do. So, you draw something on the cave walls with the primitive tools available. You have essentially created a model of the reality that you expect to see. According to the evidence, cavemen did in fact create and manipulate models!

In today's world, instead of caves, we sit in meetings, planning and strategizing what our organizations should do. Instead of drawing on the wall, we share slide presentations. Many of these slides may look slick but fail to communicate well. One of the major problems with slide decks, among others, is that the information is spread over multiple slides, and it's left to the consumer to try to connect all that information together in their head. As a result, even though the information sharing is visual, it is still disparate.

The models that you create should be clear, simple, and possibly on the same page so you can understand the holistic context of your ecosystem. You may have other models or visuals for specific parts to drive change. For example, once you realize that your skills may not be relevant in the future organization, you may have a visual to depict how you are going to acquire new skills to stay relevant in the next ecosystem.

How Steve Jobs Organized Apple

Here's another example from today's world. Before Steve Jobs returned to Apple in 1997, the company had a plethora of products that were difficult to explain. Jobs looked at all of it and suggested a simplified suite of computer products, organized to meet the needs of four different customer segments. Here's what that looked like:

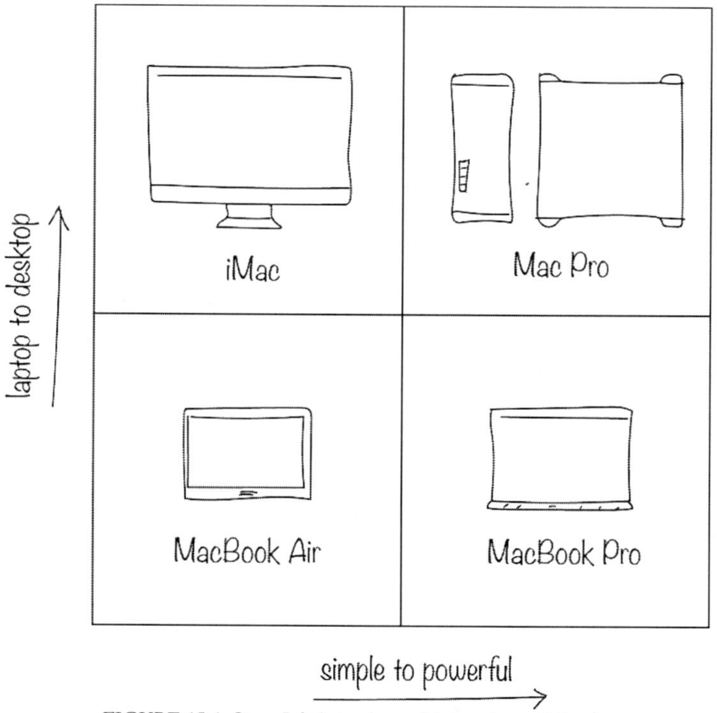

FIGURE 15-1: Steve Jobs' simple model that changed Apple

This simple picture drove Apple's strategy for the succeeding years and helped to make it one of the most valuable companies in the world. Of course, Apple introduced other products like the iPod, iPhone, iPad, and Apple Watch, but did so with strategic intent to ensure that they could interoperate with one another. Essentially, Steve Jobs helped to create an ecosystem of interconnected products. Once you purchase one product and get into this ecosystem, you buy other products, and Apple is able to hold on to you as a customer because their products work seamlessly with one another.

Never underestimate the power of simplicity!

Christmas Gifting

Here's a short video that speaks to the power of modeling—with the notion that you can model almost anything, even things unrelated to business. This video shares how you could plan to allocate your Christmas gift budget.

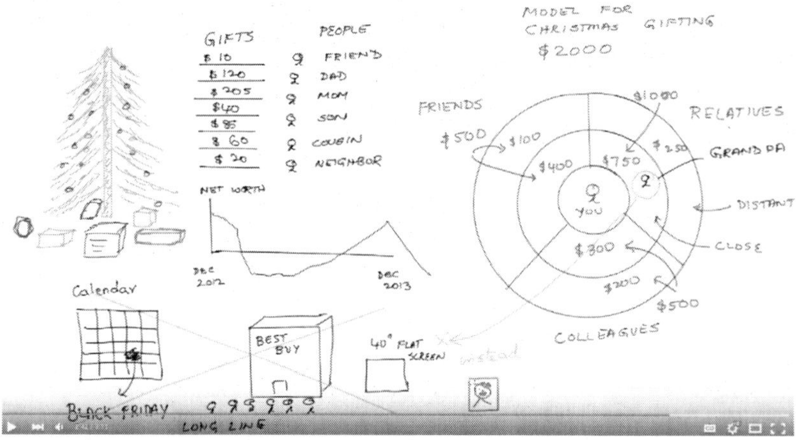

FIGURE 15-2: Video: building a model for Christmas gifting

After you finish this book, you should be able to do model virtually anything. Why do we want to model virtually everything? To solve problems. Modeling is an effective tool to understand and solve problems in our lives.

16. Analyzing and Acting on the Information

By now you know that there are different ways to model the same ecosystem. The model has to first make sense to you so you can interpret it. Always keep in mind what George Box the mathematician once said:

All models are wrong. Some models are useful.

—George Box, statistician

No model is perfect, because a model does not capture all of the information about the system you are trying to understand. Even if you were to model a piece of furniture like a wooden chair, you could not nor should you capture every detail of the chair. Even the chair cannot serve as a model of itself, because there is some metadata associated with the chair that is not part of the chair. For example, you might want to capture the maximum weight of a person who can sit on the chair, but that information is not part of the chair itself. It is external data.

We create models because we want to analyze them and make some sense of them. In this chapter I will talk about some ways to analyze models. The field of analysis is vast, so I will just introduce some common concepts and basic patterns. As you read more and come across more such concepts in different disciplines, you'll be able to recognize them as useful tools and modify them for your own use.

Model analysis is often not a separate and distinct phase from creating the model. Rather, as you spend time modeling the system, you also implicitly analyze it, which is the reason you refine your model as you go. Sometimes you realize that you are not capturing what you intended to capture and change the way you are modeling. That essentially involves analysis.

A model is never complete. As you gather more information, you should continue to refine and update it. Depending upon the information, the structure of the model itself may change, and rather drastically in some cases. You should be open to the possibility of ongoing change. As the reality that is represented by the model changes, the model should change.

Meet Your Future with Confidence

You now know how to gather information and model it in order to understand your ecosystem, so you can quickly adapt. In this critical section, I will take you through a systematic way to analyze models. This is very similar to what companies do to adapt, and I am modifying important concepts from that context so it can be applied to us as individuals.

I'll give you a structured approach for doing this exercise. The essence of this approach is to capture your current reality, think about the future reality, model your ecosystem, and find your place in that future reality. Once you've done that, your task is then to identify the skills you need to develop so you can get to that position. Along the way, many things will change. Perhaps your depiction of the future will not be fully accurate; perhaps you will change your mind on what role you want to play in the future; or perhaps some external factors will influence you to change course.

Not to worry. You will find yourself adjusting your model of the future state as you get more clarity. You do, however, have the tools to model any such future state so you can thoroughly understand it.

I'll break this process of adapting to the future into five steps. Sometimes these phases overlap, and you may find yourself going back and forth between them. That's perfectly normal.

(1) *Capture your current ecosystem:* In this step, you clearly understand your current ecosystem, your role, your responsibilities, etc. Treat it like a self-reflection phase.

(2) *Capture your possible future ecosystem:* In depicting the future ecosystem, you will need to understand everything that is changing in the ecosystem, and that includes automation, AI, customer expectations, etc.

(3) *Understand your current and future skills and capabilities:* This is where you have to take a deep look at your current skills and capabilities, and truly understand what skills you need for the future, depending on where you position yourself.

(4) *Plan on closing the gaps:* In all likelihood you will have to make an adjustment, so create a plan. Not all skills will have equal value, so you will have to prioritize.

(5) *Continually iterate:* Repeat these steps indefinitely as the future changes. I call this out as a separate step because it is as important as the previous ones. You cannot simply learn something and then stagnate. Constant adaptation and learning should become part of your DNA.

By now you know many of the modeling techniques and how to model your ecosystem. Using known information, you can model your current and future states. The question to ask next is, now that you have envisioned one or more possible future states, do you have the skills and knowledge to operate in that future?

It is best to draw two different visuals—one that reflects the current ecosystem and another that reflects your guesses on what the future ecosystem will look like. Yes, this may seem painful at first, but in most cases, the future will be quite different from the present. Understanding the present helps you get grounded in your reality, but the main focus should be your future.

If you find the right tools to draw these visuals and maintain them electronically, then you might choose to use the same picture for both, but I won't get into that. Let's start simply.

Example Context—an Insurance Company

To make this section real and practical, I will use the context of a person working at an insurance company. As I walk through this scenario, I will make some assumptions and predictions about the future. Those assumptions may ultimately turn out to be wrong. In fact, it is highly probable. However, the caveat below should always be kept in mind:

It's difficult to make predictions, especially about the future.

—source unknown

Most of us have some form of insurance—car, home, life, or health. So, at the basic level, we know how insurance works. The two primary reasons I picked insurance are: (1) we have common familiarity with it, and (2) it is one of the industries that is poised for a huge change in the near future because it has been a technology laggard.[29]

You should be able to translate the concepts that I will discuss to your particular ecosystem.

How Insurance Works

The concept of insurance can be traced back to the third and second centuries BC and was practiced by Chinese and Babylonian traders. Much of their trade was conducted over waterways, which could be treacherous at times. The traders could lose their ships or have their goods stolen by thieves. To protect against losses for any particular ship, they started distributing the risks by pooling their money and covering each other's losses.

The same concept applies in modern-day insurance, in which a group of people agrees to share risks. An insurance company facilitates the mechanics of how this is done. Let's touch upon the different roles in an insurance company that foster this facilitation.

First, the customer pays money to purchase insurance, in return for a promise that they will be covered in case of a loss.

The customer might interact with a salesperson such as an agent to

---

[29] "AI Will Transform Insurance Industry, Execs Say: Accenture Report," *Carrier Management,* May 31, 2017, http://www.carriermanagement.com/news/2017/05/31/167640.htm.

understand the product offerings and insurance types. The agent's job is to ensure that the customer has the right coverage for their needs.

Actuaries develop the models used to analyze and predict the risk and help the company decide how much to charge for coverage.

Let's say that the customer has insured their car. If the car is in an accident, they file a claim to recover the cost of the loss. In this case, the customer may interact with a claims representative who will facilitate the claims process. The claims process includes the role of an adjuster who evaluates the damage to estimate the value of the loss.

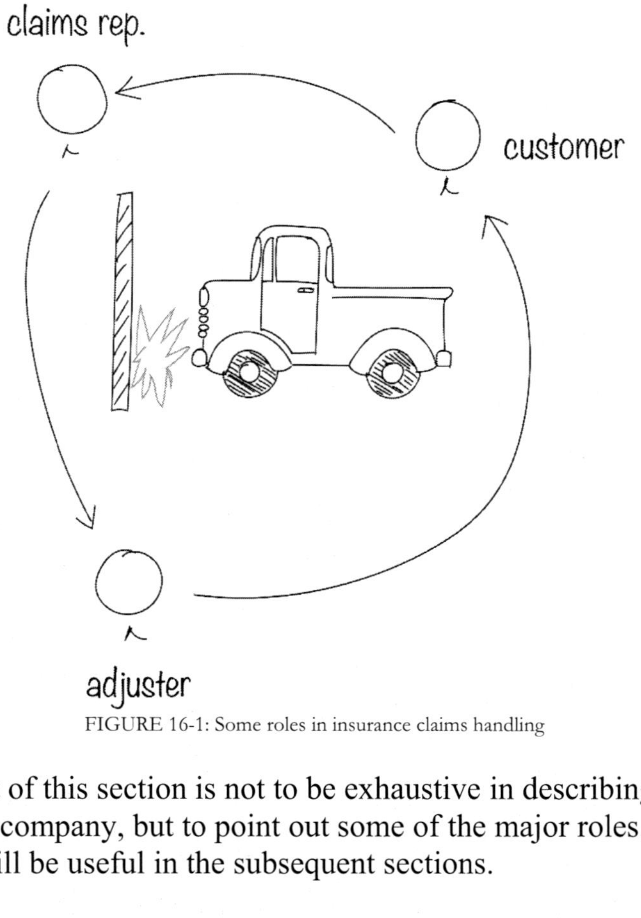

FIGURE 16-1: Some roles in insurance claims handling

The intent of this section is not to be exhaustive in describing an insurance company, but to point out some of the major roles. This context will be useful in the subsequent sections.

The following picture illustrates major parts of an insurance company. As you might observe, other businesses may have similar parts, minus those that are insurance specific.

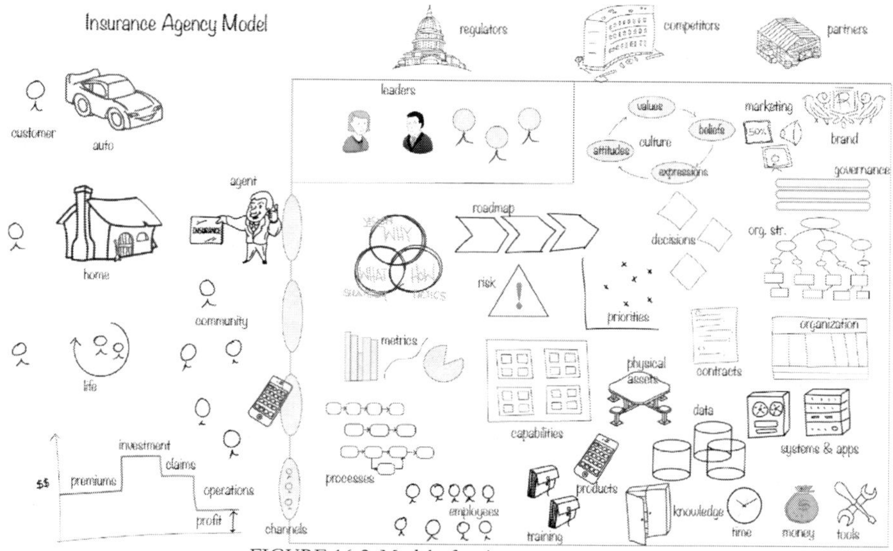

FIGURE 16-2: Model of an insurance company

The large square on the right represents the elements inside the company. On the top are external entities that interact with the company. Insurance is offered to customers through channels, and one of those channels is the agent.

This particular picture shows that the company offers auto, home, and life insurance. On the lower left is a picture that shows how the company makes a profit. It collects premiums based on risk and invests that money. It also has to pay claims and use money for operations. What is left is the profit.

This is our basic insurance company model.

What's Changing in the Insurance Ecosystem?

The following picture illustrates some of the changes happening in the insurance ecosystem. Let's take this from the top and circle around.

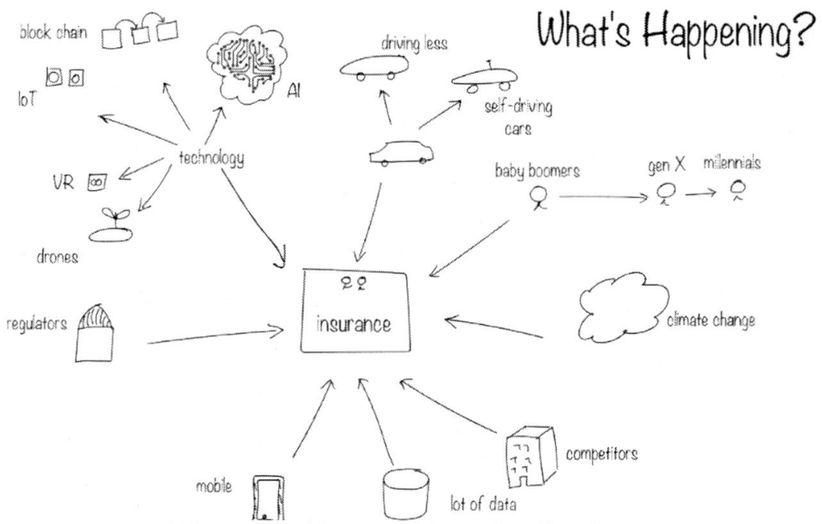

FIGURE 16-3: Modeling external factors that affect a business

First, self-driving cars may hit the roads. These cars are predicted to be safer and therefore will have fewer accidents. If this is the case, then insurance companies will have to reduce the premiums they charge customers. This in turn will reduce their overall income.

As demographics change, millennials are going to become a majority. This group is comfortable with digital technologies and more socially conscious. Many of them prefer not to own cars, so as a general trend, fewer people will own cars. Perhaps the rental car business will grow. Due to their comfort level with technology, millennials prefer to interact with companies through digital means, and very rarely will they seek the help of an agent. Where does this put the agent's role in the future?

The number of disruptive competitors in the ecosystem is growing, driven by technologies. Just as Airbnb has disrupted the hotel business, technology startups such as Root Insurance and Lemonade are disrupting the insurance business. This new class of disruptive competitors uses business models based on technology. Since many of them are starting from scratch, they can build their processes, systems, and organization with the latest technologies (one of them being AI), and leverage the latest thinking in management. These companies are proving to be flexible and adaptive.

The abundance of data is another thing to consider. Many objects, which in our case are cars, homes, and humans, are being fitted with monitoring devices. All of this data can be crunched for detailed analysis. For example, cars fitted with sensors will be able to capture data such as driving speeds, component efficiencies, places traveled, etc. This data in turn can be used to estimate insurance risks and therefore set premiums with a greater degree of accuracy.

Mobile devices are becoming the predominant way for customers to interact with companies. Their use is only predicted to grow further in the future. This means that companies will have to reevaluate their channel strategy, especially that of the agent and call center.

Finally, we come to technology. As I discussed in Part I of this book, multiple disruptive technologies will impact how business is run. This includes AI, of course, but also other technologies such as VR, cloud computing, APIs, big data, and drones. When quantum computing can show business value, it will also be added to this model at some point in the future, exemplifying how industries continue to change.

You have a specific role in your company. How would these factors impact the direction of your company, or the direction of your own job? These are questions we will try to answer.

What's Your Role and What's AI's Role?

We understand something about the influence of external factors and, specifically, disruptive technologies in the insurance industry. If you happen to be an agent, then your future may be unpredictable—purely depending on external conditions, which have nothing to do with you or your skills. Self-driving cars and changes in customer mindsets might change the underlying business model. Most future customers may prefer to purchase car insurance though their mobile devices. They will not visit you, the agent.

In that case, you will have to reexamine your role in the organization. If you build transferable skills, are agile, and are open to change, you will be in a better position to adapt. Your capability to sell products and to establish and build relationships with people might be useful in other situations.

Now let's consider the impact of AI. It enables the automation of many tasks, such as working with a large set of numbers to find underlying patterns and quickly making independent decisions based on prior knowledge. You have to identify those tasks and establish expertise in alternative domains. For example, AI is nowhere close to replicating human capabilities in communication, creativity, imagination, empathy, or leadership.

As you take a look at your current role, think about how much time is spent on the different categories of work. You might even want to log your time for two weeks to identify the categories of work you do. Here are some categories to start with: creative work (like producing new content or connecting things), organizational work (like attending meetings and managing people), and mundane work (like tracking what others are working on and updating a document).

What parts of your work can be automated or done by "smart machines"? It is often difficult to guess what smart machines can do. There is a lot of hype and there are some unrealistic scenarios, mostly derived from movies. Robots will not take over the world anytime soon. However, it is a good idea to be informed about what machines can and cannot do. If you know that, then you can develop your skills so they can complement what machines can do.

You'll first have to understand what AI is capable of doing. Only then can you figure out what your own strategy should be.

In the next ten years, here are some possible AI capabilities and limitations:

- AI will drive cars, but won't be able to console your daughter after her breakup.

- AI will find answers to customer questions, but won't be able to empathize with a customer who just lost their house to a tornado.

- AI will crunch a lot of data to identify underlying patterns, but won't be able to figure out what kind of data to feed on.
- AI will review all of the medical research to identify what treatments work, but won't be able to conduct the research itself.

If you can figure out what parts of your future job AI can do, then you can complement it by doing what AI cannot do. You can then create a plan of action to develop those complementary skills.

Here are some questions to ask yourself:

- Am I in direct contact with the customer, thereby giving me the "best view" of what the customer wants?
- Am I doing mundane things?
- What percentage of my role is creative, what part is organizational, and what is mundane?

You get the idea. With the answers to these questions in mind, here's how you can use the modeling process to adapt to your future.

Capturing Your Current Ecosystem

To start, we need to capture and understand everything that's relevant about the current situation. This includes things like your current experience and skills, where your company is heading, what you are doing now, etc.

As you can tell, this is a tall order. However, the tools presented in Part II will come in handy.

At the highest level, we want to understand our own "landscape." First, picture yourself visually in your current ecosystem. This ecosystem includes many things such as your current company, your current job, your current skills and knowledge, your current experience, your current constraints, and so on.

Let's continue with the example of an agent at an insurance company—and let's say that's you. As an agent, you might have your own business and office. You may employ some staff to help you. The primary way you make money is to sell insurance to new customers and service existing customers. You are paid in commissions proportional to the amount of business you bring in.

Say you sell the following kinds of insurance: car, home, life, and health. From a product standpoint, auto insurance is relatively simple, and the computation of its premium can be automated with machine learning. After all, we know all of the information about the customer, and all the information about the car. The main job is to feed this information into a rating table and compute the quote. The rating table was traditionally built by people called actuaries. However, with machine learning, this table can be automatically computed and updated dynamically as the ecosystem changes.

The same principles can be applied to other insurance products as well, such as home and health. A very interesting change in the health insurance industry recently was the Affordable Care Act, which mandated insurance for all people, even those with preexisting conditions. Many of the factors used to compute health insurance premiums disappeared. So, health insurance premium calculations were simplified and could be automated.

Under these conditions, what value does the insurance agent continue to offer, if any?

If you, as an agent, offer the insurance of many companies, then the value you provide to the customer is to personally walk them through different insurance plans and help them determine the best option. To attract new customers, you may do marketing, event hosting, and other activities to get your name out there. Your main job is to build relationships with customers who will potentially purchase insurance through your agency, for which the insurance company compensates you.

Sometimes insurance companies may offer incentives to you as the agent to push certain products. As a result, you may be offering customers products that are not necessarily optimal for them, but optimal for you in terms of commissions. However, modeling does not concern itself with ethical considerations. The purpose is to model what is real, not interpret rightness or wrongness. In other words, it is what it is. Having said that, the model can be used to "fix" issues that are illegal or immoral, because we can understand them after we model them.

Capturing Your Possible Future Ecosystem

In the above scenario, what does the agent's future look like?

Based on the ecosystem identified above and some of the assumptions made, the agent's role is likely to change. Commoditization makes it easy to automate car insurance, and simplification makes it easy to automate health insurance.

Life insurance and home insurance are much more complicated, since there are so many factors that affect the premiums. This means that, for now, we need an agent to collect the right information, feed it into the software, and then generate a quote. The agent can adjust the value of some of these factors and make a few assumptions to give a reasonable quote to the customer. The agent's job is to explain the quote and empathize with the customer.

Now let's reconsider the changes in the ecosystem. The millennials and the younger generation have grown up in a digital world. While they might still value human interaction, this generation does not have the patience to deal with bad human-based processes, if they really don't have to. In their minds, if something can be done efficiently and automatically, then it should be done efficiently and automatically. This is especially true of processes like having to buy insurance, which is not necessarily viewed in a positive light.

With machine learning, the purchase of complex products such as life and home insurance could also be automated eventually.

That could leave the agent out of a job in a few years. That's the harsh reality. The travel agents of yesteryear have all but vanished.

Financial advisors are being replaced by robot advisors. The insurance agent's job is similarly under threat, as are other intermediary jobs.[30]

I use the insurance agent example solely for illustration. You may be in a different role and what you do perhaps will not be automated anytime soon. Or, more likely, just like computers automate many of our tasks today, AI will help automate more complex tasks in the future and leave you with the option to focus on high-value-added work. The question, then, is what portion of your job is high value added? If you are unable to find such high value in your current role, be ready to adapt to a new role and build the skill sets and expertise to morph into it.

Modeling Your Future

Earlier I talked about how to model leadership qualities. You can use a similar approach to model your current state and your future state. Then you will know what skills you might want to focus on.

This is a visual we used earlier to model people skills:

FIGURE 16-4: Model of people's attributes

In this case, instead of using Sandy and Tim, we could use the

[30] Paul Michelman, "Don't Get Caught in the Middle," *MIT Sloan Management Review*, November 3, 2017, https://sloanreview.mit.edu/article/dont-get-caught-in-the-middle/.

"current you" and the "future you." Recognize the skills you have and the ones you'd need for a future role.

Then you should be able to prioritize the new skills and work on developing them. As an example, your ability to read a lot of information (like what today's lawyers do) and summarize it may not be such a useful skill, so you won't need to focus on it. In the diagram, that oval will shrink for future you. The skill to build strong networks with people will be more valuable, so that's an oval that will grow in your future state.

This is a visual representation of your current and future capabilities. As you learn more about your current expertise and about the needs of the future, this visual should evolve. It is not "one and done." Expect to iterate through this indefinitely.

Positioning Yourself Competitively

One hard fact of reality is that in this new world, you can't just be another body with a standard set of skills. You have to differentiate yourself among your peers. Luckily, such competitive advantage is not difficult to achieve if you combine skills.

As a simple example, if you are a mathematician, you have to be among the top one percent of mathematicians to have a competitive advantage. On the other hand, if you are passionate about music as well, and you can use your expertise in these two areas in a creative manner, then you have automatically narrowed the playing field. In other words, there will be fewer people who are experts in both mathematics and music. If you add another skill to your repertoire, then your skills can be even more unique, giving you a competitive edge.

This boils down to recognizing what your skills and expertise are, and what you should develop. It is important to figure out the value that the unique combination can provide. Simply developing multiple skills with little connection will not get you anywhere. That will just make you a jack of all trades but a master of none, which is a precarious position.

The following video explains this concept further.

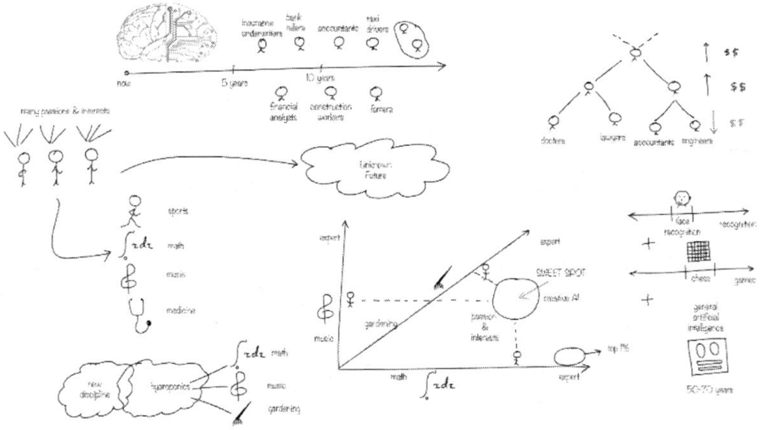

FIGURE 16-5: Video: what's your expertise?

Understanding Your Current and Future Skills and Capabilities

Going back to the insurance agent scenario, what are some of the skills you use? What are some skills that you have but do not get to use?

I will not attempt to list all the skills required for an agent, but I'll mention a few. You are able to run a business, hire employees, manage an office, sell to potential customers and understand their needs and empathize with them, use data and computer systems to compute premiums, and understand and solve problems for customers.

Your source of income is selling insurance policies to customers. You are the intermediary. If customers decide to go directly to companies that have automated much of insurance buying, then there is no need for them to come to you. This is not your fault—it's just that the ecosystem has changed, just as the advent of the web made the job of small-time travel agents irrelevant because customers were given direct control and information to plan their trips.

Given your skills, what then can you do to adapt to this change? You need to find a role that can leverage your current skills and your passion.

Again, predicting the future is a risky exercise. So, I'm going to make some simplifying assumptions about what skills will be valued in the insurance industry. Here is a short list: creativity and innovative thinking, problem solving, building relationships with customers, communicating to explain concepts, developing grand ideas, design thinking, networking, customer empathy, and the ability to see the big picture.

Notice the shift in expertise from a logical/analytical side to a more creative/intuitive/relationship side. Your work is moving from "left brain" thinking to "right brain" thinking, at least in this particular situation.

Knowing that this is the case, you can then focus on one or more of these areas that is interesting to you and deeply develop skills in that area.

For example, if you are passionate about or have always wanted to communicate better, then you will have to develop that capability. You will have to seek out jobs or roles where communication is the main ingredient.

Even there, AI will play a role. AI systems can consume and summarize a lot of information. Be aware of what AI systems can do, and do not attempt to compete with them directly. Complement them instead. For example, while AI can summarize information, it cannot tell human-relatable stories. Maybe a skill you can develop is explaining things at a simple and human level that establishes an emotional connection with the listener or reader.

You will also come to realize that putting all your skill development in one basket, so to speak, is risky because an AI system could be developed to do that particular task well. Rather, your goal is to build up a unique set of skills and expertise that you can use in combination to enhance your creativity.

A Framework for Understanding Jobs of the Future

So far, I've covered how to model your current and desired ecosystems. It is essential to understand these before analyzing the types of jobs that you might seek in the future. Then you can strategically adapt as you pursue the future that you envision.

The best way to understand jobs is to look at the individual tasks within them. Tasks are more granular and are more easily identified as automatable or not. We can put a logically consistent set of tasks together to define a new job—one that might not even exist today. We can also predict how much a particular job has a chance to be automated, given a reasonable short timeframe of, say, five years.

Today, the tasks within a cashier's job are to greet the customer, scan the items to be purchased, bag those items, accept payment from the customer, and close the purchase with a smile. Not all tasks are equal. Some tasks are big and some small; some are more important than others; some have the potential of being fully automated and some partially automated. And so on.

To see if any task is a candidate for automation, we have to consider multiple dimensions.

The first dimension is available technology. To understand how technology will affect automation in the future, consider its past trajectory. First, we had mechanical automation, like using steam engines to drill holes and dig tunnels. Then came software-based automation, like using computers to control variables in a brewery. That was followed by data-based automation, like using data to make predictions about customer behaviors. Now we are exploring cognitive automation, like having machines read volumes of legal case histories to identify precedents.

The next dimension is the predictability of the task. The more predictable the task is, the easier it is to automate. The predictability of some tasks is more clear-cut than others. A police officer's task of giving you a ticket based on how far above the speed limit you are driving is simple. A cardiologist reading your ECG to identify any heart problems you might have is more nuanced.

Another dimension is the return on investment (ROI). On a cost versus value scale, companies will automate tasks with the highest ROI. Tasks performed by cafeteria cooks, for example, can be automated, but it is cheaper to hire cooks. On the other hand, knowledge workers who make up a large percentage of the workforce do many tasks that can be automated, and also get paid a lot more than cooks. Companies will likely try to automate higher-paying jobs with cognitive technologies like AI to cut costs.

The next dimension is timeframe. Even if automation of a particular task is likely to happen at some point, when will it actually occur? In ten years, in twenty years, or much beyond that? The further we go out into the future, the more unreliable our prediction will be. For example, the task of managing projects might be automated within the next ten years, but a manager's task of motivating their team members may not be automated in the thirty years.

The next dimension is customer acceptance. Even if a task is automatable, would the customer want it to be automated? Our experiences with automated call routing have taught us that most customers still like to talk to humans who can solve their problems quickly. In some cases, humans may be wary of machines. Would you let a robot cut your hair? Probably not, because even though haircutting can be automated, customers are fearful of a robot with a pair of scissors!

The next dimension is explain-ability. Today, machines can process large volumes of data and identify patterns or reach conclusions. For this reason, government regulations may prevent or delay some tasks from being automated. When AI is introduced into society, the government usually has to offer its approval. For example, in the U.S., state and federal governments have to pass laws before autonomous cars can become legal. The same will be the case for certain legal tasks. While a machine can help to summarize a case and even make a sentencing recommendation, the law still requires a judge to give the final sentencing.

Ecosystem support is another dimension to consider. For example, shelving products in a supermarket is not easily automatable today. But in the future, supermarkets may reconfigure their shelves to make automation possible. Amazon, has already done this by strategically designing its warehouses, reducing the need for forklift operators. While full automation may be decades away, many human tasks will disappear as ecosystems are modernized.

Finally, there is the dimension of task importance. Some tasks are too important and difficult to be automated. For example, tasks such as formulating business strategy, creating innovative business models, and using technology to enable business can be aided by automation but will continue to require human ingenuity and innovation.

Now that we've explored some dimensions for automation, what does all this mean for your job?

First, you'd have to do some research and think about how your job may be impacted by automation, specifically AI. Consider all the tasks that your job requires. For each task, use the dimensions I shared above to explore the chances of it being automated and when. Repeat for each task.

The time you spend on all tasks is not equal. So, get an idea of the amount of time you spend on each of these tasks and do a simple calculation to see what approximate percentage of your job might be automated soon.

In the future, you want to have a job that has many non-automatable tasks. In your new role, you might consider having some of the same tasks you do now, or modified versions of them. In addition, you might want to add more non-automatable tasks that might require you to learn new skills.

Many of the non-automatable tasks require soft skills like leadership, communication, storytelling, empathy, creativity, problem-solving abilities, software development, analytics, design, and others.

You can define a brand new job using a combination of tasks that use your skills, your passion, your interests, and your experience. Such a job will make you unique, with a competitive advantage and differentiated from what machines can do.

You'll be off to a great start on your self-transformation to explore jobs of the future.

Please scan the QR code to watch a video on this topic.

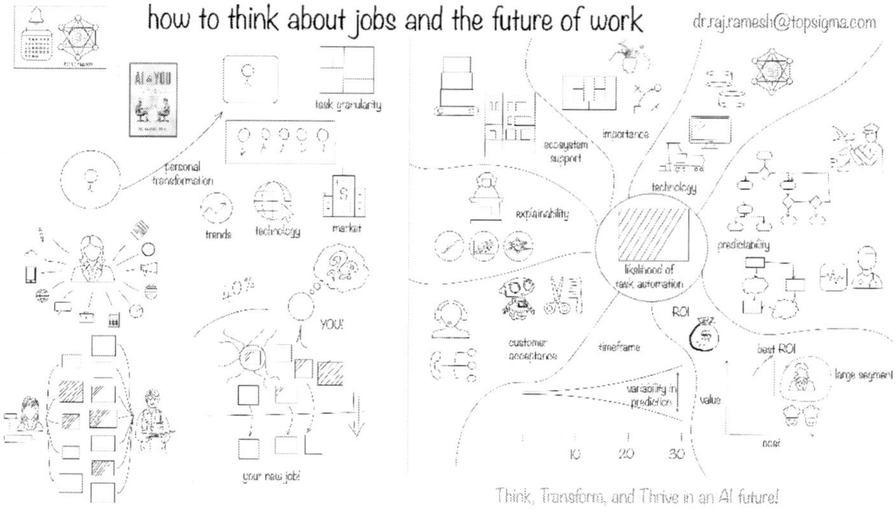

FIGURE 16-6: Video: the future of work

Closing the Gaps

Once you know what you want your future state to be and the skills required to function in that future state, then you have to identify how big the learning gap is. It may take anywhere from a few days to a few years to close that gap. Sometimes, you can close the gap quickly, but building up a high degree of expertise may require practice and more practice, as Malcolm Gladwell states in his book, *Outliers.*[31]

The figure below is a simple model that can help you visualize your current and future states and catalog the skills and capabilities that you need to build to get to the future state.

The rate of progress for different capabilities might be different because, for example, you may already be a good networker and there is not much you need to learn along that dimension. However, you may be very poor at creative problem solving, and in that case, you have to build that skill much faster. You can also choose to mature a skill to a certain point and simply stop, because that's all you need. You don't necessarily need to be an expert in all the areas you choose to develop.

This is why you don't have to be in the top one percent of mathematicians as well as the top one percent of musicians, going

[31] Malcolm Gladwell, *Outliers: The Story of Success* (Little, Brown and Company, 2008).

back to the example I used earlier. Rather, what you need is a reasonably good level of expertise that will help you build a competitive position.

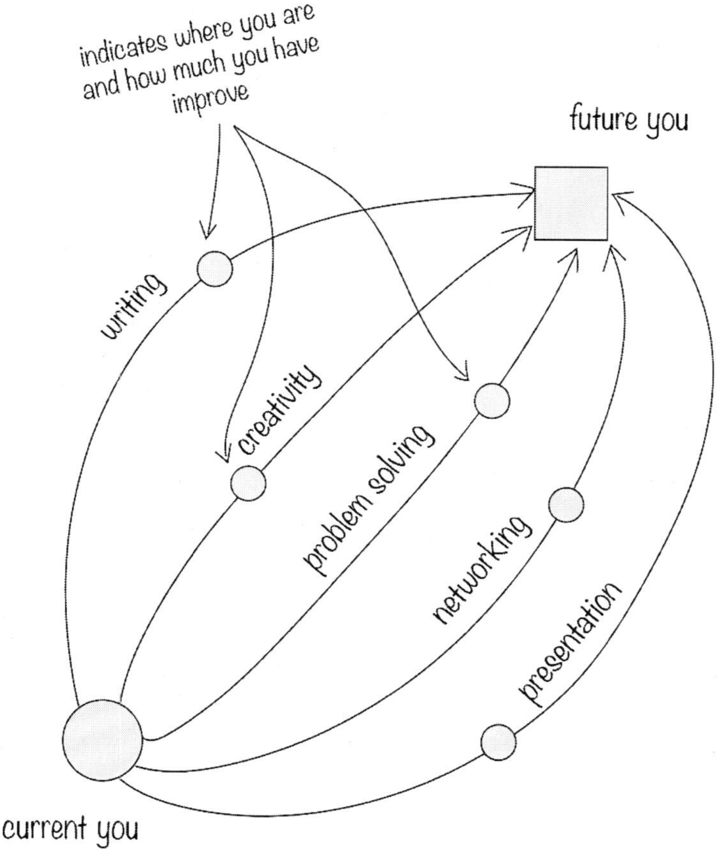

FIGURE 16-7: Mapping your current state and what will take you to the future state

Your roadmap is basically a plan to close the gap. In the above picture, we envision a future you and chart the skills and the level of each skill you'll need to develop to get to that point. You can get really fancy with this by adding any notes you need. For example, to develop your networking skills you might seek the help of your friend Josh, who is good at networking.

Keep in mind the many modeling techniques I covered earlier, to make this picture useful to you.

Continually Iterate

No ecosystem will remain stagnant. It will continue to change, and as it does, you have to remodel and readjust accordingly. I cannot emphasize this point enough.

Many times, your depiction of the future state may not go according to plan. You will have to refine and adjust many times. You might change your depictions of the future state based on learning something new. Sometimes you might even have to start from scratch. However, with the experience and skills developed in this book, you can do that exercise with relative ease. After all, you are looking to capture the complexity of your ecosystem on a handful of pages (probably no more than five 8x11s).

The ability to adapt and change is a critical skill. We often reach a plateau and it becomes difficult for us to push ourselves out. In today's world, if you are standing still, others are moving past you. If your stagnation lasts for a long time, then it will be too late to catch up. Get moving.

Always try to see how you can connect the dots of your past education and experience to establish a unique competitive advantage. Your skillset may not be unique; your experience may not be unique in and of itself; your knowledge many not be unique. For example, there are many who know how to write computer programs, many who have had years of experience in financial services, and many who have knowledge of privacy and security. However, there are few who will have the combination all three. If you can position yourself at the intersection of programming, financial domain, and security, you will have created a space in which you are unique and have a competitive advantage, not only relative to other people, but also relative to AI systems that today can only operate in narrow domains.

The key is to stay ahead of others and technology such as AI.

FINAL THOUGHTS

When I started writing this book, the audience was my children. They are teens, and I was concerned about their future. Since I have an advanced degree in artificial intelligence, I am quite aware of where machines are taking us. While there are many predictions out there ranging from Utopia to doom, nobody really knows the future. Given that assumption, I asked myself, What can I do to help my children and their children not just to survive, but to thrive in their future?

However, along the way I realized that the concepts and tools I share in this book will be useful for anyone who is likely to go through a transformation. Bringing to bear my years of experience and my perspective, I wanted to offer a comprehensive yet easy way for each of us to understand our current ecosystem, imagine the future, and most importantly, develop the skills required to thrive in that future.

By taking you through some foundational principles of how to think and how to model, I hope I have equipped you with tools that you can modify for your own needs. It is not possible to predict the future, but we have the tools to model it, no matter what it is.

Don't stop with just reading this book. Please apply the tools to your own ecosystem and create for yourself a better future.

There are no secrets to success. It is the result of preparation, hard work, and learning from failure.

—Colin Powell

Be hungry, be prepared, be optimistic.

—rephrasing Steve Jobs

Made in United States
North Haven, CT
10 November 2026

22096039R00099